REVIVAL MAN

The Jock Troup Story

by

George J. Mitchell

Christian Focus

To all the members and friends of
Inverness Baptist Church (Castle Street
congregation), whose patience has
taught me so much about grace.

The Jock Troup Story is a marvellous one, of a life committed to the service of his Lord and Master. This remarkable man was a man for all the people, and his ministry in Glasgow proved it. From one who has gained so much from the legacy he left in my own life, I can do no better than recommend this book to all, praying that the passion and fire for souls that he had for his day, will once again be experienced in our day.

BILL GILVEAR

I look forward eagerly to the publication of Dr Mitchell's book on the life and labours of dear Jock Troup.

PETER DONALD

As one of Jock Troup's 'Boys' I welcome this account of his life committed to evangelism. From the time of his conversion Jock's burning passion was to see men and women saved and his life was given over entirely to evangelism. Not surprisingly, his last breath was used to tell an audience that 'they must be born again'. I pray that a new generation will be challenged and motivated to evangelism by this book.

BERT CLARKE
FORMER VICE-PRESIDENT OF THE GUEA
FORMER CHAIRMAN OF THE TENT HALL
COMMITTEE

Photos courtesy of Andrew Carter, Glasgow.
Front Cover - Jock Troup (second from right).
Back Cover - Sunday morning free breakfast at
the Tent Hall.

ISBN 1-85792-728-1

Published in 2002
by
Christian Focus Publications, Ltd
Geanies House, Fearn, Tain,
Ross-shire, IV20 1TW, Great Britain

www.christianfocus.com

Printed and bound by
Cox & Wyman, Reading, Berkshire

Set in Garamond

Cover Design by Alister MacInnes

Acknowledgments

As any reader will probably concede, we need help when we go delving into a past we have not experienced, and I am greatly indebted to a large number of people for the help I have received. Because the contents of this book are largely social history laced with personal anecdote, my debt is to individuals as well as organizations. A few are worthy of special mention. I had good help from Mrs Rona Mitchell, Jock Troup's daughter. Andrew Carter provided valuable source material, mainly in connection with the Tent Hall. I am deeply grateful to John Fisher for lots of information about the 1921–22 Revival in the North-East of Scotland. Bill Gilvear and Jackie Ritchie were kind in lending resources. My brother Jim provided material on World War II. Alistair and Margaret Murray and Sheila MacDougall spent time and effort in reading over the text and making helpful suggestions. If I have missed anyone out, please forgive me meanwhile and let me know, so that we can include you in any reprint!

Other Helpers

The Glasgow Room (and Marilyn and the Staff of the Coffee Bar!), Mitchell Library, Glasgow.

International Christian College, Library and Archives, Glasgow.

Carnegie Library, Wick.

Inverness Public Library.

Noel Donaldson and the John O'Groat Journal.

Rev. John Adamson

Rev. Dr Crawford Ballentine

Edwin Caie

Bob Clapham

Bert Clark

Frances Cullen, Evangelization Society.

Rev. Peter Donald

Billy Dunnett

George Duthie

Rev. W.B. Forsyth

Bert Henry

Catherine McAdie

Ian McPherson

Herbie Mateer

Professor Donald Meek

Jean Mitchell

Rev. Dr John Moore

Rev. Angus Morrison

Rev. Alex Muir

Rev. David Searle

Anne Stewart

Jim Sutherland

CONTENTS

1

The Ingredients of Revival

Why is it almost eighty years since we had a real revival in mainland Britain? Are there any common factors or general principles behind its occurrence? Can we create a climate in which revival could flourish? Is there anything special about the men God uses in revival? These are the kind of issues which arise when we approach this subject, and Jock Troup, the central human figure in this book, is a good focus for our interest.

Jock Troup has never received the attention his life deserves. He was a central figure in the last two religious revivals in mainland Britain, in East Anglia in 1921, and the North-East of Scotland 1921–22. The longer we look at his life and ministry, the more we realize that we can only make sense of what the Lord did through him when we view him in a revival context. His experiences in 1921–22 and his walk with the Lord kept him in 'revival mode' for decades, always attempting great things for God and constantly expecting great things from God, like William Carey. It seems that he was the human agent God took up and used to bring a very large number (thousands rather than hundreds) of people to faith in Christ.

Therefore, our first task it to investigate the meaning of the term 'revival' and to highlight a few of its major components.

What is revival?

Since the verb 'vivify' means 'to enliven, to animate, to give life to', the term re-vival must mean 'to restore life, to re-animate', that is, to repeat the procedure of giving life. One of the prayers frequently used in connection with revival is 'Do it again, Lord!' Dr Martyn Lloyd-Jones catches the flavour when he writes:

> It is an experience in the life of the Church when the Holy Spirit does an unusual work. He does that work primarily amongst the members of the Church; it is the reviving of the believers. You cannot revive something that has never had life, so revival, by definition, is first of all an enlivening and quickening and awakening of lethargic, sleeping, and almost moribund church members.
>
> Suddenly, the power of the Spirit comes upon them, and they are brought into a new and more profound awareness of the truths they had previously held intellectually, and perhaps at a deeper level too. They are

humbled, they are convicted of sin...and then they come to see the great salvation of God in all its glory, and to feel its power.

Then as a result of their quickening, they begin to pray. New power comes into the preaching of the ministers, and the result of this is that large numbers of people who were previously outside the Church are converted and brought in.

If we can switch the imagery from that of an almost moribund body to an almost defeated army, revival is God taking the field like a Champion, or a heroic Leader, who rallies His battle-weary troops and inspires and deploys them for victory.

In simple biblical terms, revival is God rending the heavens and coming down (Isaiah 64:1), His arm (an image of efficient power) awaking and putting on strength (Isaiah 51:9), or the windows of His heaven opening and blessing pouring down upon His people (Malachi 3:9).

Revival is basically God's activity rather than man's. William Fleming defines it historically as 'Divine visitation'. Revival happens when God bursts in on the Christian scene. It is produced neither by human organization or contrivance. It can come as unheralded as a thunderstorm. Rev. Duncan Campbell, who was deeply involved in the Lewis Revival, said, 'When revival happens, you do not need to have a publicity campaign. God does His own advertising!'

Nevertheless, the most cursory studies on revival show that God uses means – and sometimes the meanest of means! This is so that 'No-one shall boast before Him' (1 Corinthians 1:29). This is the reason why God could use a man like Jock Troup.

Duncan Campbell, one of the preachers greatly used by God in the Lewis Revival, defined the state of revival as 'a people saturated with God'. There are other brief definitions of Revival, as 'God taking the field', or 'the inrush of the Spirit of God into a body that threatens to become a corpse'. Stephen Olford, whose expository ministry has been exercised mainly in America, distinguishes 'revival with a small r' from 'Revival with a capital R'. 'revival' refers to personalized or localized revival. 'Revival' refers to a thorough-going work of God which alters communities. He uses the illustration of a becalmed sailingship (the church in its unrevived state) and the responsibility of the sailors on board to set the sails so that they are ready when the wind comes. The signs of a church in dynamic tension prior to Revival are: a desire to repent, a waiting on God in prayer, and a longing for the infilling of the Holy Spirit (see Ephesians 5:18). Charles Finney believed that God was bound to react by granting revival if the conditions He set were fulfilled by His people.

The majority view represented by Jonathan Edwards is that Revival is entirely a work of God rather than a work of man. Revival is a largely unheralded, uncontrived eruption of God's presence and power among His people, which results in a significant, large-scale disturbance of their present state, a deepening of their spirituality, and a partially measurable, long-term impact of the Gospel upon the surrounding community of unbelievers. It occurs within the evangelical communities of believers, and there is often an individual or a small group of individuals at the heart of the action. Skevington-Wood writes that Revival rekindles the 'passion for souls', and turns the concept of 'the priesthood of all believers' from a privilege into a responsibility.

Genuine Revival, says Skevington-Wood, includes the following features:

- an intensified awareness of God
- jealous concern for truth
- an absorbing concentration on prayer
- an exciting realization of (evangelical) unity.

The features noted above were present when God moved in Revival blessing. Jock Troup's significance in the Christian church is, first of all, that God deigned to use him in the blessing of His people. This is an object lesson and an encouragement. Many hundreds and even thousands of people were ushered into the Kingdom of God through 'Our Beloved Jock'. Secondly, Jock Troup was a front-line soldier in the army of the Lord, in the reviving activity of God in the two revivals we have mentioned.

We can find revival principles embedded in Scripture. We do not have to go beyond the Old Testament for some schooling in revival.

Throughout her history, Israel's periods of expansion took place only when there was a power vacuum among the superpowers. Her normal role was that of political football, or land-bridge or bufferstate. The big players on the stage of history were Egypt, Syria, Assyria and Babylon. From the viewpoint of secular history the Israelites were normally 'bit players' or extras. The only exceptions to this were two periods known respectively as 'The Golden Age of the Hebrew Kingdoms', during the reigns of David and Solomon and 'the Indian summer of the Hebrew Kingdoms', during the reigns of Jeroboam II in Israel and Uzziah in Judah.

In the early years of Solomon's reign, God visited His people in a remarkable way at the dedication of the Solomonic Temple. Solomon's prayer at the dedication is recorded in 2 Chronicles 6, and the Chronicler takes up the narrative of blessing in chapter 7 verse 1:

> When Solomon finished praying, fire came down from heaven and consumed the burnt offering and the sacrifices, and the glory of the Lord filled the Temple. The priests could not enter the temple of the Lord because the glory of the Lord filled it (2 Chronicles 7:1).

This verse encapsulates neatly four of the elements of God's visitation in revival – **Prayer, Fire, Possession and Glory.**

Prayer

Most revivals are born in **prayer**, at least as a context, if not a condition. We shall attempt to demonstrate this in the history of revival. When people in need cling on to God and engage in prayer, they find that they are not wringing a response from a reluctant God. George Whitefield said, 'Our Saviour loves to let us see greater things.' God cannot be strapped into a set of conditions which in some magical way will force God's mighty hand to act in blessing. Charles Finney was a fine man of God, who knew sustained blessing throughout his ministry. However, his view that God's revival blessing comes as an almost automatic reaction to conditions being fulfilled by His people, is not generally confirmed in the historical out-workings of Revival.

Nevertheless, the special dimension of prayer has to be noted. Prayer is a futile exercise to the self-sufficient. The essence of prayer is that we have to go outside of ourselves for help. The prophet Samuel told Israel of his prayerful concern for them: 'God forbid that I should sin against the Lord by failing to pray for you' (1 Samuel 2:23). James bluntly tells believers that they do not have because they do not ask from God, and sometimes when they do ask, their prayer is well wide of the parameters of God's will (James 4:2-3).

John Livingstone was in an agony of prayer before God all night before the Kirk O' Shotts awakening on 21 June 1630. God's movement among the members of the Holy Club in Aldersgate on 24 May 1738 took place at a prayer meeting. William McCulloch's parish of Cambuslang experienced a spectacular quickening in 1742, when fifteen prayer meetings were going on regularly. The movement of God in the Nigg area of the Highlands of Scotland, during John Balfour's ministry in 1739, took place in an area which had ten prayer groups gathering every Saturday. The work of God which took place in Dundee as a result of the ministry of Robert Murray McCheyne and William Burns from 1839 onwards, stood, supported by unceasing prayer. There were thirty-nine weekly prayer meetings held, connected with the church, St Peter's, and five of them were carried on wholly by children. John Turner of Peterhead was God's instrument in the Aberdeen Revival of 1859 into the 1860s. Turner was a diminutive, dying consumptive, with a dreadful squint and a feeble voice. His only outstanding feature was a fervent prayer life which those who came into contact with him said touched the throne of God.

During the 1904–1905 Welsh Revival, Reuben A. Torrey saw a great ingathering at a mission in Cardiff. For a year before that, there had been prayer meetings going on at Penarth from 6–7am each day. James A. Stewart estimates that at least 40,000 earnest believers were seeking God in prayer prior to the 1904 Revival. J.G. Govan, founder of the Faith Mission, was a visitor and eye witness of the Welsh Revival, which he characterized as largely a prayer revival. He described a meeting he attended: 'No-one was in the pulpit, and the meeting was just open for any who were led to

17

take part. One after another, men, women and children prayed, nearly all in Welsh, but apparently with much earnestness. Hymns and choruses were started by different ones, and taken up beautifully by the whole congregation, but most of the time was given to prayer. We remained on for a late prayer meeting, and though we could understand little, we recognized in it the presence and power of God. It was a glorious time. When we realize that these meetings for prayer have been going on nightly for so long, and in so many places in Wales, it is not surprising to hear that places are being transformed, and thousands are being turned from sin to God'.

When God was moving in revival power in Wick in 1921, Jock Troup and his friends were crying aloud to God in a hulk in the harbour. During an evangelistic mission in Inverness, God's blessing came after Jock Troup and his friend Peter Connolly lay face down all night in Bught Park interceding before God for the people of Inverness. The prayers of Christine and Peggy Smith of Barvas, Isle of Lewis, who clung on to each other and to God, night after night in the 1940s, were at the heart of God's revival blessing there.

Fire

In addition to **prayer**, the feature of the **fire** of God is also part of the fabric of revival.

Fire burns up the dross, and in some cases, physical fire was used to consume the dross of a sinful past. When God moved at Karubaga in the Swart Valley in Dutch New Guinea (now Irian Jaya, Indonesia) in the 1950s, one of the first activities of the Dani tribe was to burn their fetishes in a huge bonfire.

Fire sensitizes. If you have had a burn in any part of your body, for example your finger, you will remember how sensitive to pain your finger becomes.

Fire purifies. Fire has a healing, cauterizing effect on God's people. In any true revival, God's people are manifestly more aware of sin in the Christian community, and take steps to deal with it. Confession, restitution and reconciliation were features of the Cambuslang Revival, documented by Arthur Fawcett.

Fire spreads. We shall see how any movement of God's Spirit covers the miles between communities and affects the people within those communities, in interest and involvement in the work of God. In revival, God's fire burns up people's personal agendas for living, and new priorities emerge. Time and distance, and personal comfort and decorum all go into God's melting-pot when the fire falls. In the Cambuslang Revival, people walked from Kilsyth, and further afield, because their hunger to be where God was working was so great. Howell Harris spent what he called 'five weeks in hell' before finding Christ in spring 1735 at a Whit Sunday communion service, as conviction of sin burned into his soul. People lay down on the heather all night at Cambuslang, in anguish before the Lord.

People clung on to the pillars of the church on 8 July 1741, in Enfield, New England, when Jonathan Edwards preached his sermon on 'Sinners in the hands of an angry God' (he had preached this sermon already in his home church). They explained later that they were gripped with the most awful fear of hell and felt they were slipping down into its fires, so they had to hold on to the pillars of the church. The fire of God spreading throughout New England from 1734 onwards swept at least 50,000 out of a population of 250,000 into the Kingdom of God. When the first phase of God's fire had died down, it was rekindled when George Whitefield went to Massachusetts in 1740. Like the relationship between Jock Troup and Douglas Brown in East Anglia in 1921, there was a wonderful mutual love and respect between Jonathan Edwards and George

Whitefield in 1740. Edwards wept unashamedly while Whitefield preached. Edwards said: 'Oh, how the Word did run! It rejoiced my heart to see such numbers greatly affected'.

When Robert Murray McCheyne burned himself out over ungodly Dundee, William Burns, who had been greatly used in the Kilsyth Revival, took his place. At the Thursday night prayer meeting, he invited people 'who felt the need for the outpouring of the Spirit to convert them' to remain, and about one hundred did so. The Holy Spirit suddenly possessed the gathering, which became bathed in tears, and the church was crowded night after night for months, as the fire of God fell. Often strong men cried out for mercy in the midst of the congregation.

The fire of God affected community life and even animal behaviour! It was reported during the Cambuslang Revival that there was in the community a laying aside of 'cursing, swearing, and drinking to excess'. Remorse and confession became part of everyday life, and courts and police cells became quiet. During the 1859 Revival in Ulster, those who fell before God in contrition and repentance were called 'the stricken ones'. For example, on the night of 9 June nearly 100 people lay all night in the new Town Hall in Coleraine. The building had just been completed, but had not been opened. William Gibson wrote: 'a solemn interest attaches to the beautiful building from the fact that the first use for which it was ever employed was to shelter very many poor sinners, while they agonized with God for the pardon of sin'. In Belfast, a whisky distillery was put up for auction and in Connor two pubs were closed when the owners were converted. The appetite for gambling was diminished. In October 1859 the Maze Racecourse had a crowd of about 500 instead of the usual 10,000. At the Quarter-Sessions at Coleraine in 1860 it was reported that crime had been reduced to negligible proportions. Similarly, at the Ballymena Quarter-Sessions, held before John H. Otway, assistant-barrister, in April 1860 – that is, when the revival had been over a year in existence in that neighbourhood, which was its central district – there was not a single case of indictment upon the record. At the March Assizes, 1860, for the county of Antrim, there were only five prisoners for trial, and for the county of the town of Carrickfergus, none.

In the Welsh Revival of 1904, the pit ponies must have been quite bemused at the change in their masters' behaviour and treatment of animals. The verbal and physical punishment which was part of their everyday experience suddenly stopped! When Evan Roberts was preaching around the towns of South Wales during the Revival of 1904, a miner compared the Revival to a pit explosion, pointing out that the people were impregnated with the Spirit rather than dust and methane gas! The fire of God affected people's work agendas. When the fire of God fell at Yarmouth in 1921, the teams of fish lassies (there were generally two gutters and a packer in each team) became distressed. One of the bosses called to Jock Troup, 'Come, and lead these lassies to Christ, Jock, and let them get on with their work'.

The preceding evidence illustrates one aspect of revival previously highlighted, as having 'a partially measurable, long-term impact on the surrounding community of unbelievers'.

Prayer and **fire** form two of the ingredients of revival. The third feature of revival epitomized in the 2 Chronicles 7 incident is **possession.** The *olah*, or burnt offering, means 'that which goes up'. The sacrifice offered was totally burned in the sacrificial flame of the altar, symbolizing the total consecration of the offerer to God as he identified with his offering. The sacrificial offering was given over to God as His total possession. It is typical of revivals that the Lord's people, and especially their leaders, get taken up with Him, and are enthralled with Him, and become His possession in a new way.

For John Livingstone at Kirk o'Shotts in 1630, his sense of 'unworthiness and weakness' was replaced by 'such liberty and melting of heart, as I never had the like in public all my life-time'.

For Jonathan Edwards, after his conversion in 1720,

> ...there came into my soul, and as it were, diffused through it, the sense of the glory of the Divine Being, a new sense quite different from anything I had experienced before. From about that time, I began to have new ideas of Christ...and the glorious way of salvation by Him. And my mind was greatly engaged to spend my time in reading and meditating on Christ, on the beauty and excellency of His person...The sense I had of divine things would often of a sudden kindle up, as it were a sweet burning in my heart, an ardour of soul that I know not how to express.

Jonathan carried that sense of Christ's glory and power with him for years. Charles Wesley, in May 1738 said, 'I felt my heart strangely warmed'. George Whitefield wrote: 'When God was pleased to shine with power in my soul, I could no longer be content to feed on husks, or what the swine did eat; the Bible was then my food. There, and there only I took delight'. In October 1921, after attending a meeting at the Fishermen's Mission in Aberdeen, Jock Troup had to go into a tenement building in Aberdeen and ask God to restrain His hand, afraid that his heart would burst with his sense of the presence of God.

Glory

Prayer, fire, possession are components – what else? The fourth feature of revival is **glory.** God will not give His glory to another. Glory in Old Testament terms is, basically, weightiness: in particular the weightiness of a king laden down by the rich trappings of royalty. (In Hebrew, the verbs are the heart of the language. There are two kinds of verbs: active verbs and a few stative verbs, which express a state, or steady condition. The Hebrew noun for 'glory' is derived from a stative verb meaning 'to be heavy'.) In the Old Testament, the appearance of the glory of the Lord is associated with light phenomena, or shining. For some of us, this helps to explain why God uses offbeat, bizarre individuals in revival: people who have not gone through the 'normal channels' of preparation for ministry. To that extent the 'Jock Troups' of God's church emulate their Master, in the opposition they met from organized religion.

God must have the glory, and when God shines out in revival, there is an irresistible incandescence which cannot be either explained or imitated. In revival, God trails His coat, as it were, and those who become involved will never be the same again.

In the 1949 Revival on the Isle of Lewis, there was an eruption of joy and praise among His people, so that they gave Him glory, and He showed them His glory, and this is typical of revival blessing. Duncan Campbell said he never heard the praises of God, evidenced particularly in Psalm-singing, sung like that anywhere else. A lady from Wick, Mrs McAdie, told how she walked one and a half miles to and from the school where Jock Troup held children's meetings, singing all the way. An elderly man, Robert Harper from Wick, told how 'Jock sent them home singing because God had made them so happy'. In the aftermath of revival, key figures who have given themselves in revival find themselves worn out, and bereft of the power in preaching, which God graciously granted at the heart of His reviving activity. The 27-year-old John Livingstone was greatly used in preaching at a communion season at Kirk o' Shotts on Monday 21 June 1630, when over 500 people turned to Christ. We have told how he described his state 'with such liberty and melting of heart, as I never had the like in public all my life-time'. Yet he tells how 'the following Monday, I was so deserted, I couldn't express what I wanted. So it pleased the Lord to counterbalance His dealings, and to hide from pride in man'. Similarly, Douglas Brown, the Baptist pastor who was greatly used in the East Anglia Revival in 1921, asked those present at a ministers' fraternal to pray for him because he said 'I have lost my power'.

Because of the 'ingredients' highlighted from this one Old Testament passage, we can be more aware as we explore the events of the intensified periods of God's working in 1921–22 in East Anglia and the North-East of Scotland. It also helps us to understand why Jock Troup cherished and lived in a 'revival mode' long after the events of those earlier years.

2

A Man in the Making

Jock Troup was born in 1896 in the village of Dallachy, between Fochabers and Spey Bay, at the mouth of the River Spey in Morayshire, one of Scotland's best salmon rivers. When he was about seven years old, the family moved north to Wick, Caithness, where Jock was to spend his formative years. William Wordsworth wrote in his poem 'The Rainbow' that 'the child is the father of the man', and many of the traits that were to be seen in Jock the adult, emerged in Jock the child. A few people are leaders from childhood, and Jock was one of them. He had a rollicking sense of fun and laughter, boundless energy, effervescent good health, immense physical strength, a loud voice, a commanding manner, and a great talent for engaging deep loyalties that would stand the test of time. Two mischievous boys, John Troup and his pal John McBeath, used to 'lie in wait' for the Salvation Army band passing, their pockets full of pebbles which were used as ammunition for throwing at the big drum. He was a risk-taker with a flimsy instinct for survival. Physically, he was developing the barrel chest of the sprinter, and sometimes needed his running skills to escape trouble! His acts of daring action in the watery environs of Wick almost got him drowned a couple of times during his boyhood. He almost lost his life when he fell over a railway bridge during one of his boyhood adventures. His activities were sufficiently serious to bring him up before the Wick magistrates twice.

Mr and Mrs Troup were Christian believers. Mrs Troup was a deeply spiritual lady, bearing out the old saying 'an ounce of mother is worth more than a pound of clergy'. She prayed for him constantly, and both parents did their best to bring him under Christian influences, in a strict home environment. Jock described it like this: 'Law was the order of the day and my father and mother never failed to mete out the penalty if it were broken at any time'. He longed for the day when he would be freed from so many restrictions and restraints, when he could live his life in his own way. Sunday with its full round of services and religious activities was 'a day of horror' to him and many a time he rebelled against it, but all to no purpose. But there was a service he really did love – the Band of Hope – led by one Mr Barclay. Real impressions were made here!

His parents were well known in Wick. Dad was a magical fiddle player, in the Scott Skinner mould, and mum owned a pie and tea shop in the main street of Pulteney-town. As Jock developed into manhood, his broad shoulders, barrel chest and mighty fruity voice gave him an almost quaint appearance and demeanour, like an adult before his time.

Fishing assumed a very important role in the Scottish economy. Pulteney-town near Wick had been one of three 'stations' set up by the British Fisheries Society in 1796. By 1887 the gross value of sea fisheries was £1,915,602, of which £1,128,480 was accredited to herring fishing. It was little wonder that herrings were the 'silver darlings' of Scottish folksong. The Wick production figures topped all other centres by 1855. By 1874, the year that the railway arrived in Wick, the town had slipped back to fourth or fifth in the herring 'league table'. But the town staged a comeback to some of its highest figures ever in the early twentieth century.

Steam power in the fishing boats made Wick an ant hill of busyness in the final years of the nineteenth century. From the beginning of the twentieth century, bigger engines propelled the fishing vessels. Steam drifters were three or four times the cost of the best sailboats, and they dominated the industry. The annual herring catch touched a million barrels by the early 1900s, and the North-East of Scotland had 80 per cent of the Scottish fleet (840 boats by 1914). Every steam drifter that went to sea was said to sustain 100 jobs ashore. From Lerwick to Leith, the herring industry provided great, if intermittent, prosperity. The gold rush in the herring industry was between 1895 and the outbreak of World War I. Boats were paying about 20 per cent profit on the investment made, and banks were very eager to lend money for this enterprize. The proud boast about the Wick harbour of Jock's boyhood was that it was so crowded that you could cross it by foot from boat to boat. Of course, Jock Troup had to try this out, and on one occasion, he got trapped between the boats, permanently weakening his foot and ankle.

When Jock left school, he went to train as a cooper with the firm of Flett in their curing yard on the Pulteney side of Wick. The locals had nicknames for two of the fish-curing firms – 'Guts and Shavings' and 'Sin and Misery'. This was hard, demanding work, with long hours. Coopers had to replicate the standards for barrel dimensions set out in Parliamentary legislation since the time of George III, the leak-proof demands of the fishing bosses regarding the joints in a barrel, and had to train the gutting and packing teams of three women for maximum speed and accuracy. Jock became a very skilful cooper, a keen student of human nature, and was able to use his leadership qualities to great effect. His vocal and instrumental skills were also developed: he sang and played the banjo. He pursued pleasure with great gusto, and became a fairly heavy smoker, and card-player who could curse and swear with the best and worst of men. He later gave thanks to God that he had never developed a taste for drinking alcohol.

The 1921 Revival in which Jock Troup was later to become a key figure took place mainly among the 'fisher-folk' of East Anglia and the North-East of Scotland. Revival came when there was a great economic slump. In the timing and care of God's careful providence, people were given time and inclination, in their need, to turn to God. It is sometimes said that the 1921 Revival in Scotland was a Scottish import from East Anglia – the fishing fleet brought it home with them. The evidence would rather seem to indicate two-way traffic. God was working in an unusual way, at least in pockets, in the North-East of Scotland before October 1921. The return of the fleet after October 1921 gave this work a new impetus.

Herring was the staple of the Scottish fishing industry. The so-called 'Scotch Cure' of herrings was reputedly invented by a Dutchman at the end of the fourteenth century. Wilhelm Benkels is credited with devising the technique of removing the gill and long gut, and then packing the fish in barrels, with a layer of salt between each tier of fish.

Pickled herring packed in barrels were exported to, among other countries, Holland, Finland, Russia and Germany. 'Girls' (some were of maturer years) worked in teams of three (two gutters and a packer), and could gut fifty to sixty herring a minute. 'Nae speed, nae money', was how one girl tersely summed it up. They worked outside in all weathers, their fingers tied up in rags, wearing cast-off clothes which became impregnated with fishy smells. When their fingers were cut with handling the fish bones, the salt stung their skin constantly. Rubber gloves came into use only after World War I. Until 1920, they sometimes worked from 9 am until 3 or 4 am the next morning, without meal breaks. Friends were allowed to bring them food so that they could snatch a bite while they worked, or they could send out for flasks of tea and sandwiches.

A barrel held about 900 fish, 20 tiers to the barrel, and sold for about £1.15/- (£1.75). Girls got about 8d (three and a half pence in today's currency) a barrel pre-1918. The highest rate reached 1/2d (six pence) a barrel. Average earnings were about eight shillings a week, minus three shillings for lodgings, compared to domestic servants, who earned about two and sixpence a week, all found, by the end of World War I.

Coopers like Jock Troup served a four-year apprenticeship at their trade. At the outset, their boss would issue them with a free set of tools, but required them to make him a free barrel every week, so that a time-served man would have made about 200 free barrels for his boss! Coopers had special responsibilities in training and supervising the fish-lassies, and helped in the preparation and salting of the herring. Bad gutters and bad packers could ruin a firm, for success depended on the quality of the product.

In Scotland, quality was guaranteed by the Scottish Fishery Board inspectors. Scottish fish were graded in seven categories (there were only three or four in England). The constituents and sizes of barrels, which were officially stamped, were covered by Parliamentary legislation. Officers inspected at least four out of every hundred barrels. One inspecting officer at Peterhead was nicknamed 'Bunghole Willie' because of the depths to which his zeal would extend in a barrel to catch the girls out.

When World War I broke out, Jock's foot and ankle problem ruled him out of active service in Flander's fields. He was called up and directed to the Royal Naval Patrol Service, sailing in the steam drifter *Strombo* out of Kingston Harbour, Dublin. Spiritually, he left home for wartime service feeling residual resentment for his strict upbringing. Physically, he was the picture of health and his skin glowed. A neighbour of Katie Black, who became his wife, described him to me in the following terms: 'He had huge hands. He could pick up a fully inflated football easily with one hand. He had sixteen-inch biceps, unexpanded, and a neck like a prize bull'. He belied his daunting physical appearance with a warm smile, an old-world politeness and a considerate kindness, which won him many friends. Jock formed a deep friendship with a sailor from another ship on the same patrol. His friend had a habit of getting drunk and finding trouble. Many times Jock had to carry him to the ship, and so save him from appearing before the commander.

Jock's heart was melted when Mr and Mrs West, who were in charge of the Dublin YMCA, invited him and his mate to Saturday tea, and amazed Jock by not mentioning God or the church or the Gospel throughout the meal. He had been on his guard, knowing full well that he was a prayer topic for many folk back in Wick, and was ready to show his customary resistance to any approaches. However, as they left, Jock and his friend were invited to the Sunday evening Gospel meeting in the YMCA hall in Dublin. Jock's innate politeness, the common sense and spiritual wisdom of Mr and Mrs West, and the Holy Spirit's perfect timing, converged in a positive response. The young sailor began to attend as many of the Sunday evening Gospel meetings in Dublin YMCA as his duties permitted, and came under what used to be called 'conviction of sin'. Nowadays the terminology of religious conversion has suffered a sea change, and the emphasis is on the side of human commitment rather than divine grace. The current theological terminology talks about 'making a commitment to Christ', opting for Christ, or choosing Christ as the panacea of any ills, or psychological inadequacies, so that the Gospel becomes like spiritual polyfilla for any gaps you may have in your persona. Political emphasis in recent years on the 'feel-good factor' has perhaps had an influence. Jesus makes you feel a better, happier person, so that you are more fulfilled. Thus the stress is on the need for fulfilment rather than the need for forgiveness. By way of contrast, in the Jock Troup era, Christians claimed that they were 'saved' from the punishment and consequences of sin, the fires of hell, fear of the judgment of sin which would follow death, or Christ's return, and so on.   They were 'converted', turned round by God's grace and enabled by Him to move in His direction for their lives. The Gospel preaching fulfilled the rubric of the Gospel chorus:

> Make the Book live to me, O Lord,
> Show me Thyself within Thy Word,
> Show me myself, and show me my Saviour,
> And make the Book live to me.

Consequently, faith comes from hearing the message and the message is heard through the word of Christ (Romans 10:17). The men who preached were perhaps 'unschooled, ordinary men' (Acts 4:13), but they would defend themselves as graduates of the 'Holy Ghost Bible School'. Some of them spent many of their spare hours in Bible reading and Bible study. Many of them had little formal education, but God made them into articulate Christian gentlemen with a mature faith tempered by Scripture and everyday experience in the workplace. Through their presentation of the Gospel message, God's Holy Spirit revealed the nature of God, to men and women, boys and girls, unpacked the implications of a sinful, unforgiven life, and pointed people to the Lord Jesus Christ as their only Saviour and hope. The move towards salvation was a God-induced work of gradual conviction of sin, and an increasing awareness of their need of Christ. A sense of sin can be a healthy thing because then our faith is grounded in a sense of need for God's forgiveness which, when experienced, leads to a lifetime of service given in gratitude to God. Jesus said that those who were forgiven much, would love much.

This was all true in the experience of Jock Troup. Having said to Mr West after one of those Sunday evening meetings, 'I think I'll get converted', Jock describes the aftermath in his own words:

Little did I think that God would take me at my word. Something laid hold on my life and I became utterly miserable. I tried to throw it off, but the conviction deepened. We left for patrol the next day, Monday, and I could never explain the awful misery of that week. Day and night I was like a hunted man; my sin was before me every moment. I tried to get rid of it by resolving to turn over a new leaf, but it seemed the more I tried, the worse my conscience smote me. I stopped swearing and gambling and tried to give up smoking. When none of these things could give me peace, I made up my mind I would go and speak to Mrs West whenever our time of patrol finished.

I did not wait for my chum, for my anxiety was too great. The burden had grown till it kept me from sleeping lest I should die and wake up in hell. How faithfully Mrs West dealt with me by showing me from the Scriptures what Christ had accomplished on my behalf! I listened to it all, but could not grasp the wonderful truth of it. She then prayed for me and got others to pray for me, but it seemed to me that I was beyond hope. I left the building feeling like one of the damned.

On arriving at the ship, however, I opened the wheelhouse door and got on my knees and cried to God to save me for Jesus' sake. My burden simply rolled away and the deliverance was so sweet that I rushed into the cabin to tell the crew what had happened. The playingcards were on the table as usual and members of the crew were awaiting my return to have a hand. What a shock when I told them I was saved! Some mocked and gave me a few days to hold out, but praise God He has led me on.

That night, Jock went across to another ship called the *Sparkling Star*, which was on the same patrol, and woke the skipper, an experienced Christian called Andy Duthie, and shared his good news. Andy's comment was: 'Son, you have made the greatest and finest decision anyone can make. You have a friend in me always'. Jock was to spend the rest of his life sharing Christ with others.

At the end of the War, Jock was demobbed and returned to Wick in 1919, and identified with the Salvation Army, throwing himself into Christian witness after completing twelve-hour shifts at his coopering activities. The locals in Wick recognized that he was a transformed man, the barrel-chested barrel-maker, well-equipped for open-air preaching, with a voice of George Whitefield proportions. Dr Harry Ironside, the pastor of the Moody Memorial Church in Chicago, describes his reaction to his experience of hearing Jock Troup for the first time, preaching in Glasgow in 1927: '*What a voice was his!* It was the noisiest I had ever heard, and his words came tumbling out like machine-gun fire with their rich northern accent. And his whole message from beginning to end was like a mighty clap of thunder from the Almighty God. After three-quarters of an hour of thundering forth the message with breathless speed, he suddenly paused. It was then as if we had just passed through an earthquake, the silence in the building was so keenly felt.' Rev. Peter Donald told this writer that Jock's voice could carry for 500 yards without amplification.

During the period when he served as Superintendent of Glasgow's Tent Hall, he was preaching at Glasgow Cross, and he could be heard at Lewis' (now Debenham's), *above the noise of the tramcars*. Bob Clapham recounted how someone in Bangor, Northern Ireland, claimed to be able to hear Jock clearly a mile away, along the promenade, which is fantastic volume even allowing for the amplifying effect of the sea water by Bangor beach.

For the most unusual and thrilling story about how the voice of Jock became the voice of God, we have to go to Edinburgh. Dr John Moore tells how Jock and his wife Katie were living in the cramped space of the little 'prophet's chamber' above the Carrubber's Close Mission in Edinburgh's High Street. It was the early 1930s and Jock was ministering at Carrubbers. On the Saturday night, he could not sleep, so he quietly took his key and went for a walk down the Royal Mile. He reached the bottom of High Street and the green area facing Arthur's Seat. For no apparent reason, he felt led to 'have a shout' around midnight. The preacher's huge voice went into action, booming out the words of John chapter 3:16: 'For God so loved the world that he gave His only begotten Son that whosoever believeth in Him should not perish but have everlasting life'

– towards Arthur's Seat, a landmark hill in Edinburgh. Jock felt rested, walked home and slept well. On the following night, Sunday, the Mission was packed to the door. Jock preached, gave an invitation, and was called over in the counselling room by someone who was trying to counsel a lady who had come for help. 'Listen to this lady's story, Mr Troup', she said. The lady being counselled was the foremost spiritualist medium in Edinburgh. She told how her life was a mess and she had decided to end it all. She had gone out to Arthur's Seat on the previous night to commit suicide, and suddenly she heard a voice from heaven speaking God's Word. She told how by the time the voice had finished, she was on her knees before God, and had come to the Mission for further help.

Jock was also a loud singer, and could attract a crowd and generate a fair head of steam with his banjo playing! Jock led prayer meetings in hulks in the harbour and children's meetings in a local school in the Wick area. He was a tornado of activity from day one of his return to Wick after World War I. His daughter Rona has traced his dynamism to the following cause. She pointed out that the Bible's emphasis on Christ's return does not have the place in Christian preaching which it used to have. Jock firmly believed that Christ could return any day, and so he had to 'redeem the time', winning people for Christ before the Lord's return. The emphasis on evangelism which resulted from this was paralleled by an intense interest in missionary work for a similar reason. When the Gospel had been preached to all nations, then the Lord would return, so every Christian had a responsibility to engage in mission and support missionary causes.

The news of Jock Troup's gifts spread throughout the area, and his weekends became very busy, preaching in the villages within easy striking distance of Wick. His association with the Salvation Army brought him preaching opportunities, although he was also well known and well used among Baptists and Christian Brethren. He was always smartly dressed for the open-air meetings in the Market area on Saturday nights. He sometimes wore a dressy bow tie, and a well-fitted black jacket with pinstripe trousers. He bought a car and would often transport people, especially children, in the 'dicky' at the back. The Americans called the dicky a 'rumble seat'. It was basically an upholstered boot-lid, which, when swivelled open, could seat passengers. Some of the cars of the twenties, notably the Ford Model A, were fitted with a rumble seat. Jock used it to take children to Tannach School, where he held crowded children's meetings. He taught the children homespun choruses, like:

Come to J-E-S-U-S,

And J-O-Y will follow.

An eyewitness said he told the children at his meetings that heaven was full of the sound of little children singing. These meetings were to be the forerunner of many he was later to conduct in Glasgow and Arbroath, and Bangor in Northern Ireland.

Wick was a bastion of the prohibitionist movement. The Temperance (Scotland) Act, which followed the Temperance Act of 1913, allowed localities to hold a poll on the matter of a veto against alcohol. A shortage of supplies in the Wick area made an alcohol ban easier to impose, with a well-organized and vocal opposition to drink reinforcing this. For example, they organized a concerted programme of temperance meetings and held weekly temperance services in the Breadalbane Hall on Sunday nights, led by ministers from the Baptist Church (Rev. W.H. Millard) and the Central Church in Dempster Street. The Wick Salvation Army Corps of 1920 was also in favour of a 'no licence' ticket, and a Wick Citizens' No Licence Union was formed in April 1920. Wick Salvation Army was led, appropriately enough, by Captain Dry. In the poll of 1920, 62 per cent of 2,320 voting, from an electorate of 3,013, meant that Wick was to become 'dry'. No public houses or licensed grocers in Wick were open for the sale of alcohol to the public from 28 May 1922 until 28 May 1947.

3

From Cooper to Preacher

Jock had to attend to his bread-and-butter duties
as a cooper, although work was difficult to find
in the troubled economic climate after the
World War I. The herring fishing industry was
not only labour-intensive, but migratory. The
boats followed the fish, beginning at Lerwick
in the spring and moving down the east coast,
driven by what Nancy Dorian of Pennsylvania
calls 'The Tyranny of Tide' until they reached
East Anglia by October each year. The ports
of Lowestoft and Yarmouth became a Mecca
for a great influx of Scots, who went there to
process the catch when it was landed. Special
trains at a fare of thirty shillings return (£1.50
today) were run from Northern Scotland to the
East Anglia ports.

Jock had come into contact with Holiness
teaching through his contact with the Salvation
Army and the Faith Mission. The Army had
regular 'Holiness Meetings' as an integral part
of their programmes. Both of these
organizations followed a Wesleyan, two-stage

47

approach to holiness. One of the embodiments and expositors of the Methodist emphasis on holiness was Samuel Chadwick, a prolific writer of books on personal devotion, who became Principal of Cliff College (a training facility for lay preachers), in Derbyshire in 1913. The Holiness preachers taught that there was a need for a deeper work of the Holy Spirit, separate from and subsequent to the regenerating work of conversion. The terminology varied from 'fuller consecration', 'full surrender' and 'baptism of the Spirit,' to 'the blessing of a clean heart', and 'entire sanctification'. They taught that this experience should be sought as a special anointing of the Holy Spirit, and by it Christian people were moved to have a new desire for Christian perfection, which was not sinless perfection, but would lead to a new level of undivided devotion to God, and could become for Christian workers an anointing of power for service. A few writers on this subject argued for a baptism of the Holy Ghost as a separate experience from the experience of entire consecration. There was extensive literature on the subject which was extant among the evangelical community, featuring male authors like Oswald Chambers and Paget Wilkes, and ladies like Jessie Penn-Lewis. The Holiness movement was supported by the annual

Keswick Convention meetings held each summer since the 1870s in the Lake District, where the move to promote Christian holiness was sustained by a preaching programme which encouraged Christians to put away sin and live victoriously through the Holy Spirit's indwelling presence and power. The Keswick Convention and the Faith Mission both drew their inspiration from the Moody and Sankey missions of the 1870s. The Faith Mission had been founded in 1886 by a young Glasgow businessman, John George Govan, whose family had been greatly blessed through the ministry of General William Booth of the Salvation Army. The 1904-1905 Welsh Revival's leading figure, Evan Roberts, had testified to a special experience of the Holy Spirit, and this had a strong influence on the Pilgrim Preachers who visited Wick in 1920.

On his way to East Anglia in the autumn of 1921, Jock Troup attended meetings at the Fishermen's Mission at 200 Market Street, Aberdeen. He was challenged by preaching on the subject of 'a clean heart' and 'a filled life'. Jock wanted to be his best for God, 'as holy as it is possible for a saved sinner to be', as Robert Murray McCheyne put it, and cried out to God for the infilling of the Spirit that would provide him with the dynamic for effective service for which his heart longed. Something glorious happened to Jock, so precious that he rarely spoke about it in subsequent years, and then only in hushed tones. He had to leave the meeting and he went into a tenement building near the hall and asked God to restrain His hand. Jock was so full of the sense of God's presence that he thought that his heart would burst!

News had been passed from the North-East to East Anglia that God was blessing the fishing communities there in an unusual way. The Pilgrim Preachers, whom we have already mentioned as spiritual descendants of the 1905 Revival, had seen unusual blessing in Wick in 1919. At Cairnbulg, a fishing village not far from Fraserburgh, God had graciously used the ministry of a Welshman, Pastor Fred Clarke, during the winter months of 1919. About a dozen people trusted Christ at the 'Bulgar Hall', or Cairnbulg Gospel Hall, and there was an extended period of blessing when Fred Clarke returned with George Bell in the autumn of 1921, and they preached in the villages around Fraserburgh. The families sent telegraphs to Yarmouth, telling friends about relatives who had been saved. The Lord had also been working in Peterhead, stirring people to attend prayer meetings at 6.30 each Sunday morning. When the evangelist Alex Marshal arrived from

Glasgow in the autumn of 1921, he began to experience a reaping time which was extended under the ministry of David Walker of Aberdeen, who took over when Mr Marshal had to leave.

Into this atmosphere of excitement, prayer and expectancy, a fired-up Jock arrived in Yarmouth, in October 1921.

The town of Yarmouth is situated on a spit of land between the River Yare and the North Sea, formed many centuries ago by progressive silting. It is the birthplace of Anna Sewell, who wrote the children's classic *Black Beauty*. The unattractive port area was the centre of the revival action in 1921. South of Market Place and behind South Quay was an area of congested courts and alleys called the Rows, 145 in all, set out in a grid pattern which still defines the shape of this part of town. The *Lydia Eve*, last of the once numerous steam drifter fishing boats, can still be seen periodically as a visitor attraction. The Fisherman's Hospice, a group of almshouses, is at the north-east corner of the Market Place. Nelson's statue soars above the depressing Denes area of town, on which he is doomed to gaze forever.

God's opportunity came at the point of man's extremity. The East Anglia catch was the last hope of the fisher-folk at the fag-end of a year of bitter disappointment in the industry, their 'Last Chance Saloon'. The industry had been plagued for some time with strikes and stoppages. J.L. Duthie writes about the fisherfolk:

> The patent uselessness of strikes and stoppages to improve their position by 1921, by getting the Government to repeat the guarantee scheme, or by maintaining their bargaining power with the curers, hit at their sense of their own status and self-worth.

After the First World War, the German economy could not afford to import pickled herring in large numbers. In Russia, the Bolsheviks would neither recognize debts incurred during the Tsarist regime, nor import herring, so some firms, owed huge sums of money by the Russians, went bust. As 1921 was also a bad year for gales, there was a catastrophic fall in the catch. For example, 296 Wick herring boats landed 92,156 crans worth £232,728 in 1920, but in 1922, 180 boats landed 54,925 crans worth £72,804. (A cran is a measuring unit for fresh herring, equivalent to 37.5 gallons. Fish were landed most frequently in quarter-cran baskets.) The 'John O' Groat Journal' of 4 November 1921 summed up a season of misery, reporting that some Scottish boats had left Yarmouth early, finding it impossible to cover expenses, and that more were likely to follow. The few herring which had been caught were 'lacking in size and quality, too small for either kippers or curers'. One Northern drifter, at Yarmouth for five weeks, had realized only £50. A German buyer, ready to buy 10,000 crans, said he could not purchase the small and tender herrings now being landed, and 'would wait to see if better stuff comes along... Scottish folk have little to spend'. The same newspaper also reported (11 November 1921) of the recent loss of sixteen out of eighteen crew members of a Norwegian wood pulp steamer off Lowestoft, and of 'many lives lost off France and Belgium' because of snow and frost.

Saturday evenings gave the workers a breather at the end of a week at the grind. The men enjoyed a well-earned break from the fishing until Monday, and the final phase of work for the week was completed. Adults and children relaxed in the open air, and fisher-lassies discarded their smelly working gear and went on walkabout wearing their best, knitting as they walked about in groups. In that week of general disappointment, it seemed as if the seagulls should be flying upside-down, so that they could avoid seeing the misery on that cold night on the third Saturday of October 1921.

The Christians were well catered for in Yarmouth, which had a hall in Fish Street behind the Market Place, frequented by those normally known as the Christian Brethren. The Baptist Church was tucked behind Regent Road. The Methodists gathered in the Deneside Church and Salvationists met in the Citadel beside the Town Hall. Over the past few weeks, Jock Troup and others had been preaching the Gospel message of 'our need and God's deed', at the Plain Stone in the Market Place. Several hundred people were milling about and a large number, probably over a thousand, gathered to marvel at the decibels produced by the cooper from Wick, and his riveting earnestness as he unpacked Gospel truth from his Bible. There was something compelling about the young cooper's impassioned preaching. It was as if he had caught the fire of God, and the crowds were there to watch him burning. But there was more to it than that. The Holy Spirit not only possessed the preacher. The Holy Spirit of God also came upon those who had gathered, in revival power, as He had done at odd times in the past history of the church. John Livingstone had experienced it when he preached in the graveyard in the rain at Kirk O' Shotts. More than 500 people came to Christ in that one day. Jonathan Edwards experienced it when he preached the same sermon on 'Sinners in the Hands of an Angry God' in Enfield, Massachusetts as he had preached in his own church, but when the Spirit of God fell on the gathering, large numbers of people were crying out to God for mercy. As we have explained earlier, those who were clinging on to the pillars of the church explained later that they did it to prevent themselves sliding down into hell.

Well, it was that kind of night in Yarmouth in October 1921. The text which formed the basis for Jock Troup's message was taken from Isaiah chapter 63:1ff: 'Who is this that cometh from Edom, with dyed garments from Bozrah? This that is glorious in His apparel, travelling in the greatness of His strength'. Modern preachers would have difficulty with the text. It seems to be a vision of Messianic judgment, presenting the Christ coming in judgment, wading up to the hips in the blood of His enemies. God certainly found material here that He could use. The universal verdict is that by the time Jock finished preaching, the scene was like a battlefield.

The Market Place area was littered with the bodies of those who had been felled by the Word of God and the Spirit of God. Tough macho fishermen and young fisher-lassies were gripped with the fear of God, and were crying out to God for mercy, struck down by what Rudolph Otto calls 'mysterium tremendum', and what evangelicals call 'conviction of sin'. Jock picked his way through the crowds like a spiritual Florence Nightingale, tending the wounded, trying to find peace with God for the troubled souls all around him. People were not only breaking their hearts over their lost condition before God, but were expressing concern for family and friends back home. Activities continued far into the night. The shockwaves and tremors from that meeting went on for days. Further gatherings in Deneside Methodist Church and St George's Church went on for hours at a time. Rev. Douglas Brown, a visiting minister from Balham Baptist Church in London, had been lingering on at Lowestoft and Yarmouth, and had also witnessed a mighty ingathering of people coming to Christ. Sometimes foremen would call Jock over to deal with workers in agony of soul, so that they could continue with their work. Sometimes boat crews on their way out to sea pleaded with their skipper to take them back so that they could hear the Gospel preaching. Stanley C. Griffin tells us: 'Some men were saved out at the fishing grounds, off Happisburgh, Norfolk, in an area of sea known as "Smith's Knoll". The father of Jackie Ritchie, author of *Floods Upon the Dry Ground,* which is an account of the revival among the Scottish fisher-folk, was converted in that way'.

It was nothing for Jock to be preaching for hours at a time in the open-air meetings. Douglas Brown returned to Yarmouth for the first two weeks of November, and he and Jock Troup combined in an explosive mixture of love and proclamation. Jackie Ritchie tells us that at one point in the Deneside Methodist Church, Douglas Brown and Jock Troup 'stood in the pulpit with their arms around one another, weeping as they basked in the Divine presence'. It was a holy alliance between the rough man of the North and the cultured man of the South. The revival among the fisher-folk continued under Douglas Brown after Jock had left for Scotland.

News of the events at Yarmouth spread like wildfire back to the fishing communities in Scotland, and the fishing fleet had a home-coming like never before! From Eyemouth northwards, as sections of the fleet peeled off for their home ports, the crowds gathered, and the noise of Gospel songs being sung on the boats wafted across the water. By the time the boats were tied up, the sailing choir was augmented by the welcoming choir, as they joined in singing the old hymns of the Moody and Sankey era. A whole crop of hymns in seafaring vein was born out of the blessing.

Jock had already left Yarmouth, and had reached Fraserburgh ahead of the fishing fleet. In Yarmouth he had had a vision of a man from Fraserburgh on his knees, praying to God to send Jock Troup to Fraserburgh. Jock packed up his cooper's tools, and sent them home to his mother. The tools never arrived and Jock never needed them again!

After an eventful train journey, about which the consensus view seems to be that Jock led at least some of his fellow travellers in the railway compartment to faith in Christ, he arrived in Fraserburgh and started to preach in the open air. A considerable crowd gathered, and there was a downpour of rain. Jock asked whether there was any place they could meet, and was told that the Baptist Church was open. Apparently the Fraserburgh Baptist Church deacons were meeting to frame an invitation to Jock to come and have a preaching mission there! Imagine the effect of the two groups meeting, as the deacons left the church building, and the public headed hungrily for the place where they could hear God speaking to them! Some have greatness thrust upon them! There was such an influx that the church was crowded, and one of the first faces Jock recognized in the crowd was the man in his vision, who turned out to be a Fraserburgh Baptist Church deacon, sitting near the front of the church. The sense of the Lord's presence and blessing showed that God was no respecter of geography. People could experience His electrifying presence as well in Fraserburgh as in Yarmouth. The fishermen found Him already there when they returned home.

Blessing spread along the coast like wildfire. Small communities entered into blessing. Even the secular press reflected on the impact the revival had on the communities along the coast. At this point, we shall introduce some newspaper and magazine reports of events giving eyewitness accounts from both Christian and non-Christian sources.

The Peoples' Journal' of 17 December 1921 gives an account of revival at Inverallochy and Cairnbulg, two villages south of Fraserburgh. Out of the 1500 population, it was claimed that around 600 conversions took place in a fortnight.

The Scotsman newspaper for Tuesday 20 December 1921 reported on **'Religious Revival at Eyemouth'** as follows:

At the little fishing ports of Eyemouth and Burnmouth the revival wave which is sweeping the ports in the North of Scotland has made itself felt, and nightly large gatherings meet to listen to addresses by young fishermen who have become 'converted' at the Lowestoft fishing where revival meetings are held.

It is a peculiar feature of the lives of these humble toilers of the sea (writes a correspondent) that almost every big disaster in their industry should see them, not going down before adversity, but flying to spiritual things for help. The great October gale, which robbed many a home in these ports of a breadwinner, saw a revival such as this. Perhaps not so fervent were the leaders, but nevertheless, in that dark hour the people turned to the Church. Today the men have come back from fishing at Lowestoft which has been a failure. Following upon a period of bad trade, many are on the verge of ruin, and again comes the evidence of religious feeling in the face of disaster. Ministers and lay preachers are assisting the converted orators at the revival meetings being held and though the language and phrases of the later speakers may be innocent of oratorical merit, their testimony is given with the fierceness of a north-east gale, and it is this evidence which is bearing away hundreds on the revival flood.

The *Scottish Baptist Magazine* gives a sane and modest Christian perspective in its December 1921 issue, which tells of '**Revival in the North**':

A revival is in process in **Wick**. In September of last year the Baptist Church and the Salvation Army welcomed the Pilgrim Preachers. Great interest was immediately shown, and when a month later the four Welshmen in the group returned from Shetland for ten days, a spiritual movement was beginning, but they had to leave before it could be carried further. The hunger and expectancy for revival, however, was aroused. Prayer was inspired. The Baptist Church here welcomed a deputation from the Highland Mission, who laboured for four weeks from the 20 August last, when the fishermen went to Yarmouth, and there one of our townsmen was instrumental especially in the open air in reaching a number of our young fishermen, many of them the most unlikely fellows.

The news of these 'unlikelys' startled Wick from its sleep, and when they came home and began to testify in the open-air in the Pulteney dialect, it had great power, and we believe hundreds have been converted since in the Salvation Army and the Baptist Church. There is a great spirit of enquiry everywhere. People are talking of salvation. The cinemas are deserted. The public houses much the same. Dancings are cancelled. Many years ago a Presbyterian minister called the Baptist Church the spiritual warming-pan of Wick. We feared its fire had almost gone out. But God, in answer to prayer, has rekindled it again.

The Salvation Army Headquarters have kept in close touch with the work, and have sent a number of their ablest officers to superintend it. Taking the work amongst the fisher-folk, into account, some 300 people, mostly young people, have professed conversion. Such a result in a town of some 9,000 people must have a great and abounding influence. It almost means that a new generation has been won for Christ and His service. Those attending the meetings have been largely young converts, and their overflowing joy and enthusiasm have made preaching the pleasure of a lifetime. There is a widespread religious interest in the town...there is a readiness to listen to personal talk and to receive literature...

The main problem of the immediate future concerns the new converts. What is to be done with them? There is a tendency in the North to regard church membership as a special privilege of very mature Christians. As to the fishermen converts, it is not likely that many of them will associate themselves permanently with the Salvation Army, and as a class they have not been given to church attendance...The situation calls for much prayer and careful handling...

At **Peterhead** crowded Gospel services have been held, the preachers including Rev. W. Gilmour, Fraserburgh; Rev. E.A. Bompas of London; Rev. J.W. Derwent, Aberdeen; and the pastor, Mr Horton. Thirty-one adults, besides children, came forward for salvation, and eight for baptism – nearly all folks who have been regularly attending the church.

At **Hopeman** remarkable scenes have been witnessed and the whole village is moved. Many were converted while at Yarmouth and since their return, united meetings have been held each night in the United Free Church, the minister of which, together with our own minister, Rev. S.M. Conway, conducts the services. Mr Conway writes that 'nearly all the unconverted connected with our congregation there have been gathered in. In the village all told some 140 have been converted, which, added to the seventy who professed at Yarmouth, means that the whole place is transformed, and praise of God is heard in the streets far into the night. The people are crowding to the churches. Thus, though the herring fishing has been a failure and many of the boats are home in debt there is joy and great thankfulness among the people'.

The Inverness Courier of 3 January 1922 gives an account entitled '**Jock Troup in Inverness**' as follows:

Jock Troup, one of the leaders in the revival movement, who is on his way home to Wick for a short visit, made a stop at **Inverness** last night, and under the aegis of the Salvation Army, addressed meetings in the Exchange and in Fraser Street Hall. Although his arrival in Inverness was not well known, quite a large number of people gathered and listened with interest to the life story of the Wick cooper. Troup, a stoutly built young man, speaks with a Caithness accent. He told, with no little gesticulation, how five years ago he became converted, and how the spirit of Christ had been working in him ever since, impelling him to tell his story to the perishing. He related some of the remarkable scenes witnessed at Yarmouth, where thousands were touched by the spirit of revival.

He also told of the great scenes at Fraserburgh, where whole crowds were converted. It was put down to 'emotion', he said, but it was not emotion. It was a revival in which the spirit of Christ was evident. Troup, who possesses a strong bass voice, took part in a quartette, singing one of the popular hymns. The meeting in the Salvation Army Hall was presided over by Major Flail, London, and on the platform were Rev Mr Armour, Rev. Mr Kedward, and Rev. Mr Martin of the Baptist Church.

The Christian Herald of 5 January 1922 reported:

A few additional details may now be furnished as the result of a visit I paid a few days ago to Fraserburgh, Peterhead, Buckie, etc. The movement, I can say from observation, is growing daily in fervour and intensity. The revival campaign has made great progress at Fraserburgh, where not only the fisher-folk, but business, professional and commercial men, including several of the magistrates, are taking an active part in the work....staid and unresponsive churchgoers, and even moral-living people, may be startled at some of the things said at the meetings, but I am fully convinced in my own mind that great good has been and is being done... One notable feature of the work at **Peterhead** is the large number of young men and women who have lately professed acceptance of Christ as their Saviour. Not a few of the converts, prior to the advent of the revival, lived lives careless and indifferent to all religious matters – they seldom attended a place of worship, and even openly scoffed and jeered at religion in the street and in their homes...many of these have at the various meetings publicly confessed their sins and sought salvation, and many others have given remarkable testimonies of how God has changed their lives and taken possession of them, their desire now being to lead others to Christ.

The revival in the North-East had its origin at Yarmouth, where the moving spirits of the movement were Jock Troup of Wick and Bill Bruce of Fraserburgh, both young unmarried coopers... Jock Troup is one of the leading speakers at many of the meetings, Bill Bruce usually reading the Bible lesson... The Salvation Army Hall at **Wick** proved too small to hold the crowds, and the services were transferred to the Rifles Hall. Sundays especially have witnessed marvellous and surprising scenes in the town, as many as three or four revival services going on at the same time.

Cinema houses and dancing-halls report that since the revival began their attendances have steadily decreased, and the Wick public houses are also practically empty. Customers are being attracted to the Mission Hall and the church.

The outstanding personality of the religious revival in the North-East of Scotland, without doubt, is the Wick cooper Jock Troup, a lad of prepossessing appearance, rugged and determined in style and in speech, and yet good humoured, kindly and very human withal. Jock Troup cannot lay claim to either polish or culture, and yet there is about him a quiet dignity and a pleasant manner which marks him out from the common throng. Large dark eyes relieve wonderfully the countenance, and give it a fine and even an intellectual aspect, which shows him to be a student and a man of action and purpose. Jock Troup has another characteristic – he is modest and unassuming, he does not desire publicity, and would prefer that others appeared before the public to gain approval and fame, and yet Jock Troup has been forced to the forefront by a combination of circumstances over which he had no control. The revival movement owes much to him, and as a consequence he has had to take the lead...

Criticism of the movement was, of course, to be expected, but no criticism, no amount of ridicule, can get over the fact that many men in Fraserburgh and the fishing towns and villages which line the Moray Firth, who were formerly well known to be drunkards and swearers have now given up these practices, and have become possessed of some indwelling power which gives them victory day by day over evil customs and habits... Publicans know only too well that the revival has deprived them of many of their regular patrons...

At **Wick**, a man serving behind a public bar heard Salvation Army converts singing. He went straight out of the public house and followed the singers, and was converted. On returning to the public house he packed up his clothes and gave up his job, and was immediately offered another one. In several towns the cinemas either closed down, or were half empty, whilst numerous tradesmen had to reduce their prices because they felt no longer able to make unfair profits.

The *Courant* of 8 January 1922 carries a London view of the Revival:

> It is suggestive of the emotionalism that has been more often witnessed in America than among our own people...the movement which has taken such a hold of the fishing population may not be spread to less emotional or more sin hardened parts of the country.

Mr Havers, a Hopeman businessman with no church connections wrote to the *Courant*, which published his letter on 19 January 1922:

> Having lived in this district for more than twenty years, a more level-headed class of people I have not met. Certainly they are not more excitable than the generality of people – in fact I question whether any other class would show so little excitement if called upon to undertake their dangerous employment as fishermen...if trade depression and unemployment caused this revival, surely these conditions are pretty general – and

Glasgow in particular, should soon have a big revival.

The Bishop of Norwich commenting on this movement recently, laid down the axiom that political movements in general emanate from the higher to the lower classes, while religious movements originate from the humbler classes. If this were so , Peter was one of the humbler classes and I am sure the fishing population would wish for the same effects from this movement.

At the Free Church in **Burghhead**, ninety-two new communicant members joined the church at the first communion season following the Revival.

The big coastal cities of **Aberdeen** and **Dundee** were deeply affected. The popular daily newspaper *The People's Journal* of 17 December 1921 describes how the Revival swept through the towns and villages of the North-East coast, where Jock Troup was joined by Bill Bruce and other young men in preaching the Gospel and harvesting for the Lord.

The reporter writes:

People thronging the streets are going to church; nine out of ten can be counted on being bound for a place of worship. They are not the conventional type of churchgoer. With them, religion is part of themselves, not to be confused with the donning of fine raiment. So one discovers them in the garb of their calling, the men in blue jerseys and caps, the women with shawls; but there are well-dressed people sprinkled among them, showing that the movement is not confined to the fishing class.

Where the church should hold 500, 1,000 or more have contrived to find entry and the doorway is blocked with others who would fain get in.

There is no waiting for the fixed hour of beginning. Prayer is offered spontaneously, without a break, the worship switches again into hymn choruses. Voluntary testimonies are frankly and eagerly made by recent converts. Tales of drink and gambling, of domestic unhappiness, of soured existence flow from the lips of men and women who passionately plead with the unconverted.

The message is simple. There is insistence on one point – the acceptance of Christ as the only road to salvation.

Figures in tens and twenties move down the aisle to prostrate themselves at the stool of repentance. More come out to increase the numbers of motionless figures at the front. It is an experience that sends a thrill coursing through the veins.....

The people refuse to leave the building. Once more the singing breaks out, as full throated as ever.

The story of the revival at **Inverallochy** and **Cairnbulg**.reads like a page from the ecclesiastical history of Scotland. Since the boats returned, the devotions have risen to fever heat.

At **Findochty**, some miles from Buckie, a divine spark has been fanned into a fierce flame. From 6pm until midnight, prayer meetings, conventions and processions succeed each other. Everywhere, in the home and in the streets, there is the joyous singing of hymns:

'At the cross, at the cross, where I first saw the light...'

'the revival is coming....'

The *Scottish Baptist Magazine* reports on the **Fraserburgh** revival, in the words of Rev. William Gilmour, the Fraserburgh Baptist minister:

> The larger and wider movement in Fraserburgh is related to the arrival in town of 'Jock' Troup (surely 'a man sent from God') just before the return of the fishermen and fishworkers from East Anglia. Then the little flamelets leaped up into a great blaze. The Baptist Church, where 'Jock' held his first meetings, soon proved insufficient for the growing crowds, and a move was made to the Congregational building, already opened for the overflow. Night after night and week after week witnessed the manifestation of God's power to awaken the careless and save all sorts

71

of people. In the enquiry rooms the evidences of conviction and contrition were plentiful enough. Frequent scenes of great joy there were as husbands and wives and members of the same family passed into peace and assurance through believing. Not a few who had passed through the great time at Yarmouth unaffected were found among the converts now.

During this period, almost five weeks, the reaping was constant and on a wide scale – in the meetings, on the streets, and in the homes of the people. As this was the period of 'Jock' Troup's presence and ministry, a word may be ventured concerning the preacher and his preaching. John Troup, the Wick cooper so mightily used of God, is a young man of happy, hearty disposition, natural as a child, utterly free from self-consciousness and withal wholly surrendered to God. Thrust into this work, as he himself declares, and burdened with the state of the unsaved, his soul is poured out in strong crying and tears often, for perishing men and women. His appeals are sometimes like thunderclaps, his language ready and apt; and his thought frequently striking and original. He gets his message quickly (I do not say easily), and when the time arrives delivers it with sustained energy and amazing power. God gets all the glory with this man, through whom God has spoken to the hearts of hundreds in

Fraserburgh. 'Man is a failure, Jock Troup is a total failure,' he cries, 'but Christ – He is a Living Reality'

Rev. Joseph Burns spent some days in what he called 'the revival zone', and gave a pen-portrait of Jock and the Revival:

He is not a scholar, has no tricks, no mesmeric influence to hypnotize; wherein lies his power? He is pre-eminently a man of prayer, has learned the secret of wrestling –'Lord. I winna let go till You save souls'. He copies no-one. When he comes to preach, he spends no time in preliminaries, but plunges immediately into the business of the meeting, appealing for decisions for Christ. These appeals are so urgent and persuasive, as to be almost irresistible. Notwithstanding his great popularity, he is as humble as a child.

As to the nature of the Revival, I should say that one feature is the burden of the sense of sin. Men and women thoroughly broken as they remember the past with its blots and blurs are genuinely penitent, and in the enquiry room, it was a joy to see them, of different ages, and social positions, weeping their way to the cross.

It is a Revival of Song. How the congregations sing! It is a Revival of Prayer. It is an Ethical Revival. It is making men and women new, drunkards have been converted:

young men and women who formerly were all for sport and worldly pleasure are now all for Jesus.

Rev. R.P. Buchan, **Anstruther,** wrote about the East Fife scene for the *Scottish Baptist Magazine*:

...the services of two Faith Mission pilgrims were secured, by whom the meetings were continued with encouraging results for nearly three weeks... More than sixty persons passed through the enquiry rooms, backsliders have been reclaimed, and many Christians have been greatly uplifted. We thank God that His good hand has been upon us.

In the same issue, Rev. W.J. Thomson, **Pittenweem,** reported:

The church here has experienced blessing and Revival... we have had but a small measure of the greater revival blessing which other parts are experiencing, but we continue to wait on God and expect. We are glad to say that we have the names of seventy-six who professed conversion during the past month and there are still indications of deep anxiety in the hearts of others.

The city of **Glasgow** also felt the impact. The *Inverness Courier* of 10 January 1922 reports on Rev. W.A. Ashby (of Harper Memorial Baptist Church), who had played a part in the (revival) movement in Fraserburgh and district, said that on his return to the scene of his own labours, he found a great spiritual quickening, particularly among the young men and women in the church. As an instance of this, he stated that the watch-night service lasted until nine o'clock in the morning, and those who attended it rushed home and returned after breakfast and a wash-up to attend the ten o'clock service on New Year's Day. Alluding to the revival in the North-East, he declared that it was distinctly supernatural, and in a measure had its origin apart from human agency and organization. The sovereignty of God's Holy Spirit was borne in upon him continually as he listened to the testimonies of converts to Christ, from the age of eighty-four down to fourteen years.

The *Inverness Courier* of 3 January 1922 reports on an Establishment attempt to evaluate the Revival:

The Home Mission Committee of the United Free Church of Scotland...deputed three of their number, the Rev. John Hall, of Warrender Park Church, Edinburgh, formerly minister of Cullen; the Rev. Oliver Russell, of Paisley; and the Rev. Dr

Drummond, of Edinburgh, convener of the
Committee, to visit the district and enquire
into the movement. 'We found that the extent
and character of the revival have been
exaggerated...features of extravagance have
been confined to two villages...all over, there
are evident signs of enthusiasm and often
exuberance of expression, but there is
surprisingly little excitement. To our minds
this is a genuine revival of religion, the work
of the Spirit of God. For one thing, it owes
its origin, and depends for its prosecution on
no individual leader. In different localities it
is associated with different religious
organizations or with none. The men whose
names have come to the front would be the
last to claim any credit in connection with it.
They are honest, earnest, modest, enthusiastic
young men, of sound common sense, with a
humble idea of their own ability, with a
passionately expressed love for Jesus Christ...

Those brought to decision in the revival
are predominantly young men from eighteen
to twenty-five years of age...both in the
original appearance of the revival and the
character of the meetings, there are features
of spontaneity, which deepen the mystery of
it and serve to emphasize the divine over the
human elements in it. There is indeed among
those at its head a suspicion of organization,
a determination to maintain freedom from too
fixed arrangements, for as one of the leaders

says 'You cannot organize the Holy Ghost'. Praise and prayer, along with testimony and appeal, are outstanding features at every gathering. One after another rises, sings a verse, in which all join, says it describes his experience, urges others to make it their own, or prays that the Spirit may bring the truth home to some heart...

'It is interesting to notice the light in which the young leaders regard themselves and their work. They do not pretend, nor do they feel themselves competent, to carry forward the training of young converts in the Christian life. As one of them said, 'We just gather in; they must go to others to get fed.' They advize young converts to join some church or some other religious denomination, first being sure that their choice is what the Lord intends, in order to be built up in Christian life and knowledge.

The Church of Scotland Church and Nation Report for the 1922 Assembly contained a resolution from the Presbytery of Auchterarder on the issue of Revivals:

That the Presbytery give thanks to Almighty God for the signs of revival and spiritual life in certain of the sea-coast communities and urge the Committee on Church and Nation to take the whole circumstances of the revival into earnest and prayerful consideration, with a view to determining whether any improvements in church life, work, or worship are suggested thereby.

The Presbytery...recognizes that this revival has brought to the front certain fundamental Christian truths of the first importance which are largely lost sight of in present-day Christian teaching. They, further, are concerned lest the Church, not being fully alive to the possibilities of this movement, a great opportunity for deepening and enriching the spiritual life of the church may be lost.

The matter was referred to the Home Mission Committee and the Life and Work Committee.

Perhaps it would be appropriate to round off this section with a comment on the Revival's sectional nature, and a comment on the approach adopted by Jock Troup in interpreting what was happening.

We know that the Holy Spirit is neither an influence nor a 'quasi-material fluid' as some scholars would say, into which Christians are immersed. The Holy Spirit is a Person who can be grieved, quenched or resisted, to use the terminology of the New Testament. When His work is criticized, or minimized, we should not be surprised when He withdraws His presence and blessing. As far as the English scene is concerned, Professor Donald Meek traces the success of Jock Troup and Douglas Brown partly to their experience in seafaring things as a cultural key to identifying with the fisher-folk. He also sets out a plausible case for the marginalizing of the revival movement because of the coolness of evangelical leaders like Graham Scroggie towards it. This coolness was replicated by influential evangelical groups like the Keswick Convention, which was dismissive of Douglas Brown's presentation as overly emotional when he came to take the Bible Readings at the Convention.

The Buchan Observer for 20 December 1921 referred to the powerful work being done, but its writer 'Viator' traces its source to the special psyche of being 'fisher-folk':

> Men and women, young and old, have been swept off their feet in thousands. Life has been radically changed for them; the old valuations have gone. Something big and overwhelming has gripped them: and we who stand by and gaze wonderingly, and perhaps half-contemptuously, at the phenomenon ask ourselves what it is – what *is* the force that has got to work in the hearts and homes, in the bodies and souls, of those people? – what *is* the power that has transformed our ordinary, placid, and quiet-living neighbours into praising, praying, prophesying evangelists of the Nazarene?

Now, when a man of the world reaches the crossroads of life, and finds himself in the grip of a great emotion, he instantly falls back on reason, and sets himself to rationalize his experience. He stands still and thinks...Our fisher-folk are different. They have done their thinking already. 'They that go down to the sea in ships and do their business in great waters, these men see the works of the Lord, and His wonders in the deep.' The North Sea is the temple of God's almightiness; wind and tide and moon and stars are the ministers of His omnipotence. 'Aye', said Sandy, 'He's everywhere, an' a' aroun' us; and eh, man, He gars me tremble!' Thus to the fisherman the thought of God is not new; it is his conception of God that is changed, his understanding of what the divine almightiness means to the man who is beset with difficulties and enmeshed in distresses and adversities. All that he has heard of Christ comes streaming back to him, and the Jesus of the hymn books becomes the interpreter of the eternal mind, the revealer of the love and wisdom that lie behind the inscrutable majesty of the Godhead. In a word, Christ is seen and known as the One who, as the Son, is the reconciler with the Father, the sharer of every burden, and an understanding Friend. This sense of need meets with its response; depression vanishes; the certainty deepens that whatever happens all things work together for good; and as one man after another is uplifted with a new-found happiness, an atmosphere of expectancy is created, the 'spirit of redemption' spreads; converts, burning with zeal hasten with the glad news from house to house and from friend to friend; 'testimonies' are given, prayer is offered, hymns are sung – and the revival is in being.' In the Scottish revival, it is easy to see how what J.A. Stewart called Jock Troup's 'unorthodox manner of preaching', his Northern accent, rough seafaring analogies and lack of polish and university training, grated on the sensitivities of the 'city slicker' clergymen, ensconced in their refrigerated boxes! At one gathering, someone bore down on Jock and introduced himself as 'Professor So and So from Such and Such a University', to which Jock replied, 'I'm Possessor Jock Troup, from Wick!' Jock's approach would also seem offensive. He said: 'God has chosen the lowly and humble as instruments to guide the people away from the false lights of Modernism back to the simple truths of the Gospel of Christ'.

Jock Troup would have agreed with the New Testament terms for the Gospel as:
1. The Gospel of God (Romans 1:1)
2. The Gospel of Christ (Romans 1:16)
3. The glorious Gospel of Christ (2 Cor. 4:3,4)
4. The Gospel of the grace of God (Acts 20:24)

5. The Gospel of peace (Ephesians 6:15)
6. The Gospel of your salvation (Ephesians 1:13)
7. My Gospel (Romans 2:16).

Those who heard Jock Troup preaching said that he made appeals to the hearers almost as soon as the message began, and that throughout his messages he challenged people to respond, and always attempted to have a room available for those enquiring after salvation, manned by experienced Christians. He had a team of experienced counsellors throughout the Tent Hall days. In general terms, this is in line with the classic preachers of the twentieth century. J.H.Jowett said in his Yale Lectures on Preaching of 1911: 'In all our preaching we must preach for verdicts. We must present our case, we must seek a verdict, and we must ask for immediate execution of the verdict'. Professor James A. Stewart says: 'The sinner is required to hearken and respond to the message or perish. Imbedded in the word "evangelism" is the thought of the messenger waiting to know what answer to take back to Him by whom he was sent. The Gospel cannot be ignored...the messenger of God must not be content merely to preach a delightful sermon. He must breathlessly await an answer to God's ultimatum'. John Stott states : 'We must never make the proclamation without then issuing an appeal.. we are to find room for both proclamation and appeal in our preaching if we would be true heralds of the King...It is not enough to teach the Gospel; we must urge men to embrace it'.

In theological terms, Jock's Gospel preaching would be Arminian rather than Calvinist, theology filtered through a man on fire, with the preacher pleading, often tearfully, that the hearers should respond to the Gospel. Perhaps Jock was a Calvinist on his knees and an Arminian on his feet. Whatever we make of him, he epitomized what preachers often say, that the Lord is not so much interested in our ability, as our availability. Jock was gifted in many directions, and had fine character qualifications which were signs of grace in his life - honesty, sincerity, holiness, passion, commitment. The prominent feature was that Jock was available to God, one of the 'Cry aloud and spare not' school of preachers, ready to go to great lengths so that God would be glorified and sinners would be saved. So many of our modern Christians cannot resist the temptation to arrogate glory to themselves. God was able to trust and use Jock because he always gave God the glory for any spiritual blessing which came his way.

4

Studying in Glasgow's Bible Training Institute

Some of the Christian leaders who had come to know Jock shared with him their concern that he should receive some systematic Bible training for his future ministry. He talked with the Salvation Army leaders he knew, and shared his fears that he could not fit into the mould of their kind of training. He engaged in evangelistic activities in Glasgow and Dundee around this time. After much prayer and discussion, Jock entered the Bible Training Institute (BTI) in Bothwell Street, Glasgow, where he studied (on and off) for two years, from 1922–24. The Bible Training Institute, and especially its Principal, was to play a major role in shaping Jock Troup.

The Bible Training Institute had been built in the aftermath of the Moody mission in Glasgow in 1874, when many young men and women with rudimentary education had come to Christ, and were eager to be trained for His service. D.L. Moody was a Chicago-based shoe salesman who had become an evangelist. Moody was one of a large family from Northfield, Massachusetts, whose father's alcoholism brought early death for himself and much misery for his family. Young Dwight had been greatly used in Chicago, although he always had critics snapping at his heels. He told one critic of his evangelistic method: 'I prefer my way of doing it to your way of not doing it!' He is reported to have said when asked about the great things God had done through him: 'He has had all there is of me'.

D.L. Moody saw huge blessing when he visited Scotland in 1874. He modestly gave credit to Scotland's Christian heritage by saying that the fruit was all there, and all he had to do was shake the trees. At a meeting in Ewing Place Church, Glasgow, in February 1874, 101 young men responded to Moody's appeal. David J. Findlay, later to become pastor of the Tabernacle near St George's Cross, Glasgow, was one of them, and claimed that it was 'a modest estimate to say that tens of thousands of men, women and children were "born again" in those months.' (January until May 1874).

The Bible Training Institute was the East Wing of a massive tri-partite structure which dominated the north side of Bothwell Street between West Campbell Street and Blythswood

Street in Glasgow. The central part of the building, the Christian Institute, was built first in 1878–79. The West Wing, which contained a restaurant and bedroom accommodation for 189 people in the Young Men's Christian Association, was added, with the BTI in 1895–98. The architect, John McLeod, drew his inspiration from the Reformation and designed the building in German Renaissance style, with statues of John Knox and William Tyndale above the entrance, and carved heads of other Reformers decorating the front of the building. The BTI section in the East Wing was funded largely by Lord Overtoun and his sister Mrs Margaret C. Somerville. Lord Overtoun had made his money in the manufacture of chemicals, and he and his sister gave generously and sacrificially for the work of God at BTI.

BTI was built primarily to provide education for the converts of the Moody mission who had only basic education, to prepare themselves for full-time Christian service, for example, in city mission work. For decades, BTI was the only Christian college in Britain which offered single study-bedrooms.

The Principal of the Institute when Jock Troup joined the student body in 1922 was the godly Dr David M. McIntyre, formerly minister of Finnieston Church, Glasgow, from 1891 until

1915, and son-in-law of the godly Andrew Bonar, with whom he served for fifteen months at Finnieston, in Glasgow's dockland, until the senior man's death. Dr McIntyre accepted the invitation of the Directors of the BTI to be its second Principal, and from 1915 onwards he became minister emeritus at Finnieston, and turned his total energies to the training of students. His successor Dr Davidson described him as 'an ideal chief of staff'. He was a very sympathetic man. One of his favourite phrases was, 'I'm sorry about that'. He was described at his ministerial jubilee in May 1936 as 'an Evangelist approved by God, as a Scholar and Theologian skilled in the deep things of God, as an Organizer of prayer circles among the people of God, and as a Writer whose helpful books have attained a wide circulation'. Even the most casual glance at his photograph shows a face of strength and dignity. D.M. McIntyre was one of the few evangelicals of the early twentieth century to make a clear statement in favour of Biblical inerrancy. Although there was a fraternal link between BTI and Moody Bible Institute in Chicago, he refused to embrace pre-millennialism, and was aware of the risks his college's reputation ran with those who followed American Fundamentalists in this doctrine about the last things (pre-millennialists believe that Christ's coming will precede a millennium of His kingly reign on earth). Someone said of D.M. McIntyre: 'we could never get him to denounce anyone'.

His patience was about to be tested by a ubiquitous student who was totally committed to evangelism and noisy prayer meetings! An old joke about evaluating ministers said that if they had a shiny seat on their trousers, they were men of the study, if they had baggy knees on their trousers they were men of prayer, and if they had worn-out shoes, they were good pastoral visitors (if they had all three, they needed an increase in stipend!). In Jock's case, he went to BTI with seriousness of purpose, but he never sat down long enough to shine the seat of his trousers. Nevertheless, the godly and scholarly Principal had a profound and lifelong influence on the young revivalist. D.M. McIntyre later spoke with affection of Jock's influence on his fellow students on matters relative to revival. James Alexander Stewart comments:

> It was not easy for a Principal who had to conduct a steady schedule of study to allow prayer meetings by the students which lasted far into the night, or even all night through!
> Many stories are told of those days with holy delight by fellow-students. One

outstanding one is of a time when Jock had first arrived. He had gathered some students into his room for prayer. When Jock prayed, it was the prayer of a man assaulting the Throne, not meekly asking God to do something. He prayed as he preached; with his whole mind and body as well as with his heart and soul. The chair on which he leaned rocked back and forth, while the toes of his shoes continually bumped the floor with heavy thuds as he cried unto the Lord with a LOUD VOICE. His praying and the heavy 'amens' of his friends could be heard over the entire building. On such occasions sleep was impossible for the other students, and often they were kept awake far into the night. It was during one of these prayer meetings in Jock's bedroom that a gentle knock was heard at the door. There was no answer. Then the knock became a loud rap. A voice from within was heard to shout, 'Lord, keep the devil out! Keep the devil out, Lord'. Whereupon the door quietly opened and Principal McIntyre walked in!

Another story from Jock's student days concerns a group of three young men who had travelled from the North of Scotland to Glasgow to visit Jock. When they came up the steps into the entrance area, Principal McIntyre met them and asked how he could help. They asked to see Jock Troup. The Principal said, 'Oh! He'll be doing his Hebrew studies!' He reacted to their nonplussed expressions by telling them to go out of the main door and turn left, then turn left again and continue up the hill until they met a young man with a banjo and a crowd around him. The Principal said, with a smile, 'That'll be Jock Troup doing his Hebrew studies!'

We noted earlier Jock's talent for forming strong loyalties which stood the test of time. During his time at BTI, Jock became soul-brother to Peter Connolly, and a friendship was forged from the first day they met which would be a blessing to both men, and to the advance of the Gospel. It is a sad reflection on the sick society of the present time that the 'David-and-Jonathan' kind of friendship which existed between Jock and Peter has to be explained and even justifed. In his book *The Four Loves*, C.S. Lewis in his discussion of the Greek word 'storgia', meaning 'affection', links it to the kind of relationships which existed among what C.S. Lewis calls 'the hairy old toughs in Tacitus' (veteran soldiers in the Roman Army). In Christian terms it is a warm and hearty affection and friendship in the Lord which has no shady or sexual overtones. Peter Connolly sets the scene in his own words:

Jock and I first met in the classroom of the Bible Training Institute in the city of Glasgow. That very morning we had private prayer together in his room. After we arose from our knees and shook hands, we became brothers in Christ, fellow-workers for God, and life-long comrades. For over three decades he was my nearest, dearest and staunchest friend.

On one occasion, Jock and Peter complained about a certain lecturer who had not mentioned Jesus Christ in his lecture. The Principal asked for their notes and they told him that they had disposed of them. He took time and patience to explain to his over-zealous students that the lecture had been on the Children of Israel in the Wilderness!

It may be helpful to give some details about Jock's 'playmate'. Peter Connolly was a wild Geordie gangster with Irish Catholic connections, who had been tamed by the Lord Jesus Christ. He had been brought up in one of the poorest housing areas in the harbour area of Sunderland known as 'the Barbary Coast'. Drink and fighting were the natural order of things in the Connolly household, and when he was twelve – while a raging battle was going on in the house – Peter grabbed and downed a three-quarter pint bottle of whisky, which left him in a terrible condition. He was a confirmed drunk by the age of fifteen, delivery boy and sampler for the family's alcoholic requirements.

He joined the Royal Irish Regiment, and became the crack boxer and the crack desperado of the Regiment, serving time in Army jails at Gosport, Stafford and Cork. He could not resist the temptation to steal and sell Army property, like blankets, shirts and trousers, to fund his drinking habit. His major problem was existing without drink during his periods of detention. During a fifty-two day sentence once, he and a cell-mate used a bed as a springboard and took a flying leap through a cell window, not knowing that it was two storeys up. His cell-mate was killed and Peter was carried back into captivity, unconscious.

Although the First World War ended on 11 November 1918, the end came suddenly, and hostilities continued until the last gasp. On Sunday 10 November 1918, while attempting to find an outpost, and under heavy shellfire, Peter's commanding officer was shot down. Armed only with a trench axe, Peter dashed out into No-Man's-Land and brought in the fallen man. He woke up in hospital with his dying officer lying beside him riddled with bullets, and he himself wounded. For this he received the regiment's only distinction – the Military Medal.

Jesus said that the dog sometimes returns to its vomit, and the sow that is washed to its wallowing in the mire. After leaving the Army, in the two years after the end of the Great War, Peter rejoined old friends in 'The Cage Hill Gang'. His stamping ground with the Gang in Sunderland was the Ballast Hills, great mounds of sand used for filling bags with ballast in the days of the wooden sailing ships. The Cage was a collection of buildings there which had housed punishment cells, and was a favourite haunt of fighting men, gamblers and pigeon-fanciers. The Cage Hill Gang stored their coal and contraband, and hatched their nefarious plans in the 'Ducket' (dove-cote, or pigeon-house), a more socially acceptable title for their den of iniquity than 'The Cage', giving the impression that they were merely pigeon-fanciers. Peter Connolly's gang was not a bunch of mischievous youths. They were a dangerous menace, of real concern to the neighbourhood and the police force.

Some brave Christians from the Hallsgarth Mission in Sunderland took on a prayer and practical burden for the Gang. They gate-crashed the Ducket and started Bible classes among the Cage Hillers! On 1 March 1920 Peter Connolly went with Mission folk to a Gospel meeting in Bethesda Free Chapel and at the end of the meeting he rose from his seat, walked down the aisle and fell upon his knees, yielding his life to Christ as his Saviour and Lord. In 1922 he went to BTI, and formed an immediate, deep and lifelong friendship with Jock Troup.

Peter wrote this about his evangelistic partnership with Jock:

> We have spent nights in prayer together and together we have laboured in evangelism. We have known experiences when our faces were flushed with victory, moving in the flames of true revival, seeing men and women in hundreds under the converting influence of the Gospel. On the other hand, we have known periods of leanness of soul when the battle was tough and the situation called for an all night of prayer. More than once this battle in prayer has taken place in a field and not in a bedroom. In the days of the Scottish revival, I have seen my friend weep so long and so uncontrollably that his eyes were like balls of fire as he went into the pulpit.

Peter and Jock became evangelists after their time at BTI was completed. The Apostle Paul set out the main features of Body Ministry within the church of Jesus Christ in Ephesians chapter 4:11–14:

It was He who gave some to be apostles, some to be prophets, some to be evangelists, and some to be pastors and teachers, to prepare God's people for works of service, so that the body of Christ may be built up until we all reach unity in the faith and in the knowledge of the Son of God and become mature, attaining to the whole measure of the fulness of Christ.

In his book *Body Life*, Ray Stedman draws a series of helpful analogies between the main features of our physical bodies, and the main ministries described in this Ephesian passage. To paraphrase and summarize what brother Ray has to say, the **Apostles** are skeletal and foundational within the church, like the basic bone structure of a human body. The **Prophets,** who were the preachers, challengers and encouragers within the Early Church, are like the communication systems of a human body, like neurons and nerve-ends, passing messages out from the head (brain) to the muscles and body parts. **Evangelists** in the church may be compared to the digestive system of the body. Our digestive system does an amazing work within the body. As new material – food – is introduced to the body; the digestive system converts this unlikely material in order to give the body vital flesh and energy. Under the sovereign direction of the Holy Spirit, this is the role of the evangelist. Through the word of the Gospel, God takes unlikely material, hell-bound sinners, and the whole direction of their lives is altered when they are born again by the Holy Spirit of God, and incorporated into the body of Christ. Genuine evangelists are especially gifted and anointed for this specialist task of evoking a response to God. To complete the picture that Paul paints in Ephesians 3, **Pastors and Teachers** (or better still pastors-teachers, because the same, single definite article in Greek covers the two nouns) approximate to the lowly but necessary cleansing functions of the body, the role fulfilled by the liver and kidneys, evacuating impurities and maintaining the body in a healthy, poison-free state. In spiritual terms, this is not to deny that there can be a multiplicity of functions. Pastors, for example, may also be gifted evangelists. In our era some tele-evangelists have, so to speak, 'brought the game into disrepute' by their antics. Some so-called evangelists unashamedly promote themselves rather than the Lord Jesus Christ and his Gospel. There are some money-grabbing carpet baggers, charlatans, smash-and-grab, hit-and-run men, with big expense accounts, who like comfortable hotels. Someone has cruelly paraphrased our Lord's teaching by saying, 'by their suits you shall know them'. But we don't give up using money because there is a little counterfeit about. The Ephesians 3 passage highlights the precious and specialist gift that evangelists are within the church. They are rare and vital, and should be treasured and valued highly within the church of Jesus Christ.

Ever since the Yarmouth events, and certainly after his Bible Training Institute training, Jock Troup was a rare combination of revivalist and evangelist, set on fire by God so that the world and the church could observe him burning for the remainder of his life in Christian service. He had been on God's battlefield. He had seen the raw power of God's sovereign Holy Spirit striking people down and bringing them to Christ, and the vision stayed with him for the rest of his life.

After his times of training in BTI, Peter Connolly engaged in years of fruitful evangelism and pastoral work, before going to America as a Bible College Professor – Dr Peter Connolly at the Baptist Bible College in Springfield, Missouri, USA! See what God can do! What a bunch of 'liquorice allsorts' the people of God are!

Although he was a Bible College student, Jock was in great demand as a revivalist preacher, and the time off he took to conduct missions meant that he could not be given a regular certificate on completion of his course. The Principal was very wise in his handling of his young firebrand. He gave him good counsel and loads of encouragement. Dr McIntyre wrote the following letter of commendation in his own handwriting when Jock left BTI:

Bible Training Institute
64 Bothwell Street
Glasgow.

17 June 1924

Mr J. Troup was a resident in the Bible Training Institute during part of two sessions. We enjoyed having him with us in the house – his influence over the other students was good. He took his share in our class work and in the meetings arranged in connection with the work of the Institute. We wish him every blessing in his Master's service – all happiness and much prosperity.

David M. McIntyre, Principal.

Jock and Peter often missioned together in the years during and after BTI. In the month of November 1922, Jock Troup and Somerville Smith held a Gospel campaign in Inverness, which was evidently blessed, as Jock Troup and Peter Connolly returned in December 1922.

When they were in Inverness, they stayed in a boat on the Caledonian Canal. They agonized in prayer together, on their faces before God all night in the Bught Park, Inverness, that God would give them a breakthrough, and bless the ministry of the Word with signs following in the lives of the hearers.

The preaching had its amusing side. On one occasion, Jock was ministering in what was known as the Queen Street Church in Inverness (now in use as Chisholm's Funeral Parlour). The pulpit area enjoyed much velvet cushioning, and Jock Troup was what some people call 'a Bible Thumper'. He was also a pulpit thumper, and his vigorous presentation of the Gospel raised great clouds of dust! He sweated profusely when he preached and was given to wiping his brow as he proceeded. The reliable eyewitness account was that at the end of his message, he looked as if he had just come up from a shift in the coal mine, more like a miner than a minister. There was an unholy rush to remove the dust before the second night's preaching!

Peter Connolly functioned not only as Jock's friend, confidant and prayer partner during the BTI years, but also as his Agony Aunt in matters of the heart. Jock had considerable difficulty in grappling with romantic issues, and Peter proved to be a tower of strength in this area.

After his time at BTI, Jock returned to Wick. He did travel a lot on preaching missions, some of them in partnership with Peter, but he was able to settle his heart, after some agonized thinking and praying, on Katie Black of Wick, as the wife the Lord had for him for the years ahead. Katie had been converted during the visit of the Welsh Pilgrim Preachers to Wick. The Black family came from the Wick area. They lived in the end cottage of a cluster of four, at Stirkoke, about a couple of miles out of Wick, off to the left on the Thurso road. The author interviewed Mrs McAdie, who remembered Jock passing her home in Stirkoke on his way to 'coort' (court) Katie Black. The Blacks had a woollen mill at Stirkoke and a shop in town. Their main product was woollen blankets, produced in red and grey for the Army during the First World War. They also produced tweeds from knitting yarn.

The 1928 wedding photo shows the bride's father John Black, Jock Troup and his father Harry, Katie's brother Alex, Mrs Troup and Mrs Black, and the bridesmaid Miss Thomson, who was Alex Black's girlfriend. The family had suffered a recent bereavement, so decided to go away from Wick for the wedding. The service was conducted in the Columba Hotel, Inverness, by Dr D.M. McIntyre, Principal of the Bible Training Institute.

After BTI, Jock was much in demand as a preacher all over Britain, and spent some time in a special role with the Kirkcaldy Gospel Union in Fife. Jock and Peter often travelled together in Gospel campaigns around Britain. In many of the fishing towns around the Scottish coast there are still those who remember missions being conducted by Peter and Jock. He was very popular in Ulster, and went to Bangor, County Down, first of all in 1926. He went for twelve or thirteen years to Bangor, and held large children's meetings as well as Gospel Campaign meetings for adults. Latterly, the meetings were held in a hall built during a W.P. Nicholson Convention. Peter and Jock also missioned in Portstewart, County Antrim.

From 1928 onwards, Jock was involved in the Lord's service in Kirkcaldy, based on the Gospel Union. He and Katie bought their first home in Kirkcaldy, and settled into the routines of marriage. Katie was back home in Wick in January 1929, and their first child, Rona, was born in her granny's bedroom. The Troup's second child, Betty, who was to become the pianist of the family, was also born in Wick, in October 1931. Through all this, God was preparing his young servant Jock Troup for one of his greatest tasks for Him. The call came in 1932 – from the Tent Hall, Glasgow.

5

The Tent Hall – 'Flagship of the Fleet'

This chapter aims to show that the Glasgow where Jock made such a major impact was a city with a strong evangelical emphasis. We shall set out some of the evangelical work that was going on in Glasgow in places other than the Tent Hall, and show how the Tent Hall was up and running, at the centre of a wider work, long before Jock came on the scene.

The Tent Hall in Steel Street, Saltmarket, was the 'flagship of the fleet' among Glasgow's mission halls, and the hub of the work of the Glasgow United Evangelistic Association. It had been built in the aftermath of D.L. Moody's mission in 1874 in a huge marquee on Glasgow Green, hence the name 'Tent Hall'. Features of the later, 'ameliorative' work of the Tent Hall, notably the 'Sabbath Morning Free Breakfast', had been instigated by D.L. Moody. He saw the pathetic plight of the homeless around the marquee on Glasgow Green, and said something must be done for them. Christians have always been constantly active in helping their fellow human beings, even before we had Social Work Departments. Jesus said something about it in His teaching parables, like 'The Good Samaritan'.

The Glasgow *Evening Citizen* newspaper describes the Tent Hall as 'a commodious block of buildings at the corner of Saltmarket and Steel Street', built in 1876 at a cost of £17,000. A report in 1907 states: 'For this property the Association are largely indebted to the late Mr Alexander Allan, its first President, and to Mrs Allan'.

There were huge kitchens, used constantly for the preparation of meals, especially for Glasgow's poor people. The building had a spacious main auditorium, with upper and lower levels, with the seating on a gentle slope, and slender pillars to maximize the view from the upper area. There was no escape from Gospel attack! Those who glanced surreptitiously towards the clock could not help but see the text above it: 'It is Time to Seek the Lord'. The text behind the clock read: 'Jesus is Coming! – Perhaps Today!'

The Tent Hall was an ant hill of evangelistic activity, involving very large numbers of people. It was significant that those who were actively involved in its worship and service were known as 'the workers' rather than 'the members'! There were prayer meetings galore, especially the Friday night prayer meeting for the weekend's work, rallies on Saturday and Sunday evenings, a Sabbath Morning Free Breakfast (for up to 1,800 adults every Sunday), a Poor Children's Sabbath Dinner (for up to 1,000 children every Sunday), a major weekly open-air meeting at Glasgow Cross, several back-court open-air meetings, tract bands, and a plethora of other activities enmeshed in the work of the Glasgow United Evangelistic Association. A notice of appeal for support issued by the Glasgow United Evangelistic Association in 1907 on the death of Lord Overtoun, contains the following report of the work: 'The work in the Tent Hall is devoted to the poor and is divided into two branches, Amelioration and Evangelisation. The Ameliorative work embraces what has been known since 1874 as the Free Breakfast, the Poor Children's Sabbath Dinner, the Poor Children's Day Refuges, the Poor Lads' and Girls' Help, and more recently, the Cripple Children's League, which has on its register over 1,600 cripple children. These agencies have been successful in seeking, finding and helping the very poorest in the city in the most practical ways possible.

Striking statistics could be furnished, both of the extent of the work and its fruitfulness, and we can safely say that in the course of the thirty-four years in which the work has been carried on in the Saltmarket, thousands of lives have been redeemed and raised from the lowest depths of degradation to positions of honourable citizenship, and in many cases to posts of responsibility.

The Evangelistic work in both the Tent Hall and the Bethany Hall covers the preaching of the Gospel to the poor on week evenings and on Sabbath evenings, with conjoined Saturday evening temperance work on a large scale. In each of these halls there is a vigorous 'Men's Own' Meeting held on Sabbath afternoons, and numbering respectively 1,000 and 500.

The Tent Hall is the centre of the well-known Fresh Air Fortnight movement, which under the Association has twelve beautiful Homes at various coast and country places. These Homes are entirely free of debt and have accommodation for about 800 children. During the year 1907, 7,902 fortnights were enjoyed by poor city children. There are also other similar helpful agencies carried on in connection with the Tent Hall.

The work sustained the Biggart Memorial Hospital Home at Prestwick for cripples, where remedial surgery was carried out for children with rickets. Large numbers of Glaswegian children were malnourished, so that the city had produced a higher-than-expected proportion of what were called 'wee bowly bachles' (diminutive bow-legged, misshapen people). Rickets causes malformation of bones, especially the leg bones, through malnourishment, particularly calcium/phosphate deficiency. The Cripple Children's League also had Industrial Centres and Social Parlours. The Weary Workers' Rest was at Dunoon. The Mothers and Babies' Rest was at Saltcoats. The Annual Reports of the Glasgow Poor Children's Fresh Air Fortnight and Cripple Children's League were issued under the title 'Seek and Save'.

This was a programme calculated to satisfy any evangelical activist, and change the hymn about Sunday from 'O day of rest and gladness' to 'O day of zest and madness'! Families could spend most of each Sunday in Tent Hall activities.

Imagine what it must have been like for women brutalized in a cold home with few comforts, or homeless drifters who had been living by their wits on the streets all day, to come into the Tent Hall. These were the days when only one room in a normal working-class home had heating of any kind. Carpets, or even rugs, were scarce, and the walls between the houses seemed paper-thin. Noise echoed from houses which had no linoleum, only bare boards, and family members seemed to be crowded into tiny homes. The struggle to keep going was grim and real. Thursday – the day before pay-day – was particularly grim. Wives used the services of pawnbrokers, scrap-metal merchants and salesmen at the Briggait or the Barrows to raise enough money to make it to Friday. Some wives had to meet their husbands at the works gate on Friday before the week's wages made their way into the coffers of bookmakers or publicans. Husbands often gave their wives a pathetic housekeeping allowance in order to feed the men's habit for drinking, or their hobby of attending football matches. Some men allowed the wife and children to go without good clothes so that the 'head of the house' could turn up well-dressed at the pub or the football ground. A few men went to ridiculous extremes. One man made his wife produce ten cigarettes a day out of a pathetic housekeeping allowance. Another man falsified pay envelopes, and his wife got a terrible shock when he dropped dead on the bowling green and she found out how much he had really been earning. It all added to the misery of home life for the working classes. (The author writes from a childhood of experience at the receiving end of this!)

The Tent Hall was a haven by contrast – warm, bright, comfortable, welcoming – with lovely music being created live by expert musicians playing on finely tuned instruments, well-practised choirs, and the 'cream of the crop' of preachers from home and overseas. Was it escapist? Certainly, and who wouldn't want to escape the harsh reality of life in a city which sometimes seemed more like a jungle? Some sociologists attempt to make a case that the enfranchisement of women and the Labour movement gave women a new, liberated status in society. This was not the whole story for women who attended the Tent Hall. Many of the women who attended the Tent Hall dreaded weekends and the New Year period, because of the drunkenness and debt they entailed. For men also, there was a dignity and respect given to them by Christian workers which did not have to be earned by heroic drinking, vile swearing or physical violence. Special provision was made for the people at the Christmas/New Year period, and glossy brochures advertising top preachers and singers were produced. The Hogmanay Supper for the Poor was a highlight, when the Tent Hall was filled to capacity, and Glasgow's Lord Provost frequently accepted invitations to be chairman.

In 1933 the Tent Hall celebrated Peter T. McRostie's Semi-Jubilee as Superintendent. He had trained at the Bible Training Institute, and had served for seven years prior to 1908, as Superintendent of the Bethany Hall, Bridgeton. In Churchman's report in the Glasgow *Evening Citizen* he writes about Mr McRostie's 'breezy humanity and glowing evangelical zeal'. He quotes Mr McRostie: 'Christ and Him crucified – that's our offer, and we give it straight from the shoulder'. Churchman describes Mr McRostie as 'Big and burly in frame, vigorous in personality...one of his assets, particularly in open air work, is a great strong voice, which he has never been afraid to use to full effect. Up until recently, he led many a march through the streets, and he was familiar, especially in Argyle Street and the Saltmarket, as the man who could walk backwards at the head of a procession, singing and speaking with all his might, and never missing a step.' (The subsequent biography of P.T. McRostie was entitled *The Man Who Walked Backwards*).

The other large mission hall run by the Glasgow United Evangelistic Association was the Bethany Hall in Bridgeton. (The work began in Sister Street in 1875, then in Bernard Street from 1876, and in the final years in the YWCA premises in Muslin Street.) It was a fine, open building, with no internal pillars, seating 1,500 people. It was generously gifted to the GUEA in January 1903 by James S. Napier, the ship builder, who subscribed to the teaching of Jesus that giving should be secret, so he gave the Hall with the stipulation that his name should not be mentioned in minutes or reports.

There were many other Mission Halls in the city. Grove Street Institute was a massive structure located in one of the poorest areas of Glasgow, near Garscube Road, and did a splendid Gospel and social work among the poor. Grove Street Institute had a fine Gospel Silver Band.

Glasgow also had a flourishing City Mission work, with halls as far apart as Coalhill Street in Camlachie, the Wyndford Hall in Maryhill Road, as well as a thriving work in Govan. Glasgow City Mission had been the first City Mission in the world, founded in 1826 by David Naismith, who, unable to secure the mission field of Africa, it was said, found an alternative Dark Continent up Glasgow's closes. (David Naismith was also the founder of London City Mission, London Female Mission, the British and Foreign Mission, and many kindred institutions in many towns in England, Scotland, Ireland, the Continent and America.) Having used the word 'close', this is perhaps the place to explain its meaning in Scottish terms. In England, a close is generally a cul-de-sac (often in a leafy suburb). In Scotland, a close is a narrow passage or alley or covered entrance leading to the back of a house, or to a common stairway in a block of flats.

The Tolbooth Mission was a flourishing concern, and there were a series of specialist mission halls, some of which were built to cater for particular areas of life when Glasgow was at its zenith as a port, a railway centre, and a key industrial base for the British Empire. There were, for example, Railway Missions in Maryhill (Cumlodden Drive), Springburn (Vulcan Street), Townhead (Tennent Street) and Oatlands (Logan Street).

Artizan's Hall (known locally as 'Munzie's Mission' because it was founded and led by him) was built in 1891 in the Kelvinhaugh area (Teviot Street). Carrick Street Mission had connections with the Finnieston Church. When D.M. McIntyre attended the meetings there, the people used to point him out, and say in hushed tones, 'that's the Doctor'. Paddy Black's Mission, and the Douglas Children's Mission in the Plantation district, did a great work in the south side of the city. There were Carters' missions in Spring Lane in the south side of the City, and in Maryhill Road in the north-west of the city. There was a flourishing Foundry Boys' Mission in Tharsis Street, Garngad, near Blochairn Steel Works. The Seamen and Boatmen's Friend Society had a Mission Hall in Port Dundas from 1869 onwards. Its aims were 'to promote the social, moral and religious welfare of Seamen and Canal Boatmen'. Its 1883 report cites, among other activities, 160 open-air meetings, and over 5,000 visits made to seamen, and 12,000 pieces of Christian literature distributed. It also voices 'the desirability of a new Mission Hall'. The Canal Boatmen's Institute which replaced it was located in the Port Dundas area. It was neither large (the main hall seated about 270) nor expensive (it cost £3,000 to build). It was a striking building, demonstrating great imagination in its use of its corner site, with an attractive, well-proportioned clock tower, modelled on that of the Old University, with the ogee cap common in Scottish seventeenth- and eighteenth-century buildings. Scholars have discovered within the last generation that although John Keppie was the architect, there is definite evidence that the young Charles Rennie Mackintosh, his junior, had a major influence on the building. The fine, open-timber roof of the hall was clearly his work, and it is also known that he produced the design for the clock-face. This was, sadly, not enough to spare the building from demolition in 1967 to make way for the northern section of the Glasgow Ring Road.

There were specialist missions for seamen in Glasgow, near the River Clyde, notably the Seamen's Bethel in Eaglesham Street (architect R.A. Bryden, designer of many of Glasgow's religious and charitable buildings, and friend of William Quarrier), built in 1883 to cater for sailors landing on the south of the River Clyde. It had recreation and coffee rooms on the ground floor, and a chapel seating 500 upstairs. The Bethel had a Gospel Silver Band. The Seamen's Chapel, in Brown Street, Anderston, was north of the River Clyde, and had extensive halls and a large chapel area. The building was erected by the Glasgow Seamen's Friend Society, which had its headquarters in the Broomielaw. The Church of Scotland Lodging House Mission in East Campbell Street did a valuable work for the homeless and the destitute.

The Gorbals Medical Mission was founded in 1867 to do medical missionary work among Glasgow's poor, to encourage a missionary spirit among medical students, and to support the training of medical missionaries. The first building was put up in the Havannah, a notorious black-spot near the city centre. In 1879 a hall and dispensary were opened in

Moncur Street. In 1883, the Hall and Dispensary were moved from Moncur Street to Oxford Street in the Gorbals, although some work continued in Moncur Street. These dispensaries were open at regular hours on weekdays, and an evangelistic service was held on Sunday evenings.

The northern part of the city had Mission Halls in Braid Street, Bardowie Street, Possilpark (known later as 'Allan's Mission') and Lambhill. D.L. Moody visited Possilpark in 1874 and preached in an open area in Bardowie Street, on the site where the Mission Hall was later built, from the back of a farm cart. The fourteen-year-old boy who looked after the horse while Moody preached was John McConnell, who later became one of God's 'trophies of grace' in the district. The Lambhill Evangelistic Mission Hall was an extension of a work begun as an outreach ministry by the Maryhill United Presbyterian Church. There was also a group known as 'shop-front' missions, the most durable of which was in Duke Street (it continues in High Street). During the Depression years, many of the mission halls held meetings especially for men out of work, called 'Muffler Meetings'.

Therefore, the city was a very busy place in terms of evangelical activity, and the work of the Tent Hall was a long-established one by 1932, when Jock Troup came on the scene as Assistant Superintendent. A report on the work of the Glasgow United Evangelistic Association (GUEA) on 29 May 1907 claims the following :

> Tent Hall, Saltmarket – Accommodation 2,000.
> Aggressive Evangelistic and Ameliorative work carried on continuously.
> Sabbath Morning Free Breakfast– Average attendance, 1,800 adults.
> Poor Children's Sabbath Dinner – Average attendance 1,000.

The illustrious gentlemen at the head of affairs in the early years of the twentieth century as Directors of the GUEA included the Rt Hon. Lord Overtoun of Overtoun House, Dunbartonshire. He made his money in the manufacture of chemicals, and he and his sister gave generous amounts towards the building of the massive tri-partite structure in Bothwell Street, Glasgow (YMCA, Christian Institute and Bible Training institute.) Lord Overtoun conducted what was considered the biggest Bible Class in Scotland (400–500 attending), on Sunday evenings in Dumbarton United Free High Church.

Sir John H.N. Graham, Bart, Larbert House, Larbert.

Sir Joseph P. Maclay, later to become Lord Maclay, who was very kind to the Tent Hall work. He was Shipping Controller during World War I, a task of pressing cares and exacting demands.

Honorary Vice-President Alexander Sloan, CA and another Director Hugh Brown had the designation 'CA', which stood for 'Commission Agent' rather than the modern 'Chartered Accountant'. The term 'Commission Agent' had nothing to do with the horse racing fraternity. It referred usually to a merchandiser who was involved in the profit from business transactions. Alexander Sloan ran a wholesale warehouse in the city centre.

Robert Gourlay, LLD, JP, was the Dean of Guild for the City of Glasgow, a Justice of the Peace, and Manager of the Bank of Scotland in Glasgow.

John King was also a Justice of the Peace, a Councillor for the Cowlairs district of Glasgow, and a Director of the Canal Boatmen's Institute.

By 1924 they had been joined by James S. Napier of Napier and McIntyre, Iron Merchants, William Sloan of the shipping firm of William Sloan and Co., Robert Simpson the draper, and John Steel, shipowner.

A 'Noon Meeting' was organized every Monday in the Christian Institute, where there was a guest speaker, often a distinguished preacher who had been visiting the City at the weekend. The main agenda, however, was a series of reports on the 'The Weekend's Work', when Christian leaders reported on what God had been doing in different ministries around the City of Glasgow. There was an air of eager anticipation about this meeting as news was given of souls saved and lives transformed. Sometimes, in the warm and eager atmosphere of the Noon Meeting, the reporters got carried away in the arms of hyperbole, which helps to explain why Jock Troup's nickname for the Noon Meeting was 'The Feast of Trumpets'.

6

The Depression Era

On his arrival from Kirkcaldy in 1932, the Glasgow that Jock Troup found was in a sorry state of disrepair and poverty, with an unenviable reputation for slums, disease and crime.

Victorian Glasgow had been run like a civic state, in which the Corporation was in charge of everything from trams to telephones. It became the Second City of the Empire by the late nineteenth century. Its flowering came as a nineteenth-century, Victorian achievement, in contrast to its great rival Edinburgh, which flourished as an eighteenth-century, Georgian achievement.

Glasgow is probably the only city in the world with a prayer as its civic motto: 'Lord, let Glasgow flourish by the preaching of Thy Word, and the praising of Thy Name'. The Gospel City of the evangelists became the Social Gospel City of the reformers of the late Victorian period, a huge showpiece of Christian enterprise. The city sustained a population of over a million until the late 1960s.

Glasgow was also Workers' City, although the well-heeled sections of its population tried to perpetuate the sham that the city rested on something other than the narrow industrial base of heavy industries like coal, steel and shipbuilding.

In the early twentieth century, Glasgow became the victim of a 'double-whammy'. The disappearance of the munitions market at the end of the First World War, and the ripple effect of the Wall Street Crash meant that Glasgow shared the fate of other European cities. Very large numbers were thrown on the unemployment scrap-heap. The Scottish collapse after World War I was largely due to the Edwardian economy, which had too many resources tied up in its staple industries. The city became a victim of its own success. To give one example, by 1913 Clyde shipyards launched one-fifth of the total world tonnage. By 1920 pig-iron production was at one-third of its pre-war level.

By the 1920s the city was in inexorable decline. T.C. Smout writes about 'appalling social deprivation', and 'unspeakable urban squalor, compounded of drink, abuse, bad housing, low wages, long hours and sham education'. Unemployment in the West of Scotland exceeded 25 per cent. To use Ian

Crichton-Smith's graphic phrase, there were idle men on the street corners 'chewing the fag-ends of a failed culture'. The image of Glasgow for the average Englishman was set by the ballet *Miracle on the Gorbals*, reinforced by A. Macarthur and K. Long's book *No Mean City*. The razor gangs depicted in that book reflected economic breakdown; they were adults reacting to unemployment, poverty and boredom, rather than reckless youths. They posed no genuine threat to the general public, and fought each other on territorial rather than ethnic and sectarian lines. The Gorbals gangs were less threatening than the gangs of the East End of Glasgow, where sectarian factors were stronger. The Billy Boys of Bridgeton boasted they could raise 400 men. Other gang titles included the Sally Boys, the Norman Conks and the Baltic Fleet.

People could escape from the grim realities of the Depression years, if they could afford it, by going to the Alhambra, or one of the other eleven theatres in Glasgow. The vast, warm, darkened cinemas provided another escape route, where people of one culture could bask in the dream-world of another culture. Some of the best movies ever made were released in the Thirties – Westerns like *Stagecoach* and *Dodge City* (1939); Musicals like *Swing as We*

Go starring Gracie Fields (1934) or *Top Hat* (1935); or *The Wizard of Oz* (1939); or the new crop of Horror movies, like *Frankenstein* and *Dracula* (1931), starring Boris Karloff and Bela Lugosi respectively, Fredric March's *Dr Jekyll and Mr Hyde* (1931); or Basil Rathbone's Sherlock Holmes in *Hound of the Baskervilles* (1939); and the classic War movie *All Quiet on the Western Front* (1930).

If lack of money kept them at home, what kind of homes did the Tent Hall folk come from? The majority were working-class people from the tenements around. It is wrong to paint a totally black picture of the tenements. Some people rush to complete the equation 'tenement equals slum'. Glasgow had (and still has) lots of beautiful tenement properties, with a fine red- or honey- sandstone exterior, bay windows, skilfully crafted ceilings with fine cornicing and moulded centre-pieces, and tiled ('wally' in the vernacular) closes. The rooms in Scottish tenement buildings were generally more spacious than in English cottages. A four-storey Victorian tenement in Glasgow could contain five large houses of six or more rooms, or on a building plot of the same size, twenty-five single apartment houses.

Unfortunately, the worst situations were highlighted in the Press. The *Glasgow Herald* of 15 March 1924 quoted the impressions of William Bolitho, an English visitor who wrote a series of articles for *The Outlook*. He described a Glasgow back-court in the following terms:

> As dark as the bottom of a Highland gorge. Growing in the corner against the face of the sombre backland, as straight as a monster pine, is the turnpike stair, a circular stone turret, in the centre of which winds the only stair to the scores of rooms within. Near it is an open stone penthouse, roofed with broken flagstones under which are three rubbish bins. Cats and children are pursuing their mysterious plans on the loosely cobbled floor. 'This is the back green', I am told.

Bolitho's third article posed the questions 'What deepest misery may overcrowding like this mean? What ultimate torment is reserved for humanity deprived of air, light, food, money and space? I must answer "the slum smell". In most cases the inhabitants may not notice it any longer, have grown used to it like beasts in their cave'.

Glasgow had attempted various solutions to its housing problem, which was exacerbated by the influx which followed any crisis elsewhere, like the Irish potato famine in the 1840s. In 1866 the city had introduced a system of 'ticketing' houses as a determined attempt to prevent overcrowding. All houses of three apartments and less, and not exceeding 2,000 cubic feet were measured, and their capacity, along with the number of occupants allowed by law (on the basis of 300 cubic feet for everyone over eight years old) was fixed to the door. By the 1880s Glasgow had 23,228 ticketed tenements, housing about 75,000 residents, about one-seventh of the city's population.

Many of those who attended the Tent Hall lived in the city centre, in Glasgow's most popular style of house, the single end. Despite the title, single ends were most generally found, not at corners or ends of passageways, but in the centre of a tenement landing containing three houses. The front door of the single end opened into a tiny lobby about four feet square, with a press, or cupboard, on one side. There was rarely an internal W.C. provided. A second door opened into the apartment, which usually faced the street. The outer wall had a window, with the sink and the range. The low cupboard, high shelves, and the coal bunker were placed on the side wall in front of the door. The bed recess was fitted into the space behind the door, adjoining the landing. The built-in bed was about two feet six inches above the floor. The space beneath it was often used for storage, and often contained a 'hurley bed' for children, so-called because it was wheeled, or 'hurled' out at night. During the day, the bed recess was hidden from view behind a closed door, until the door was forbidden by an Act of 1900.

By 1910 legislation made it uneconomical for private builders to continue building houses for rent. Improved garden suburbs were built from 1920 onwards in Riddrie, then Mosspark and Knightswood. The Depression forced the City Fathers to turn their attention again to cheaper forms of housing, building three-storey tenements with houses of three, four and five apartments, faced with artificial stone. The housing picture was grim throughout Britain. By 1933 there were around 400,000 homes deemed unfit for human habitation, housing some two million of Britain's residents.

Building new houses, however, did not solve the problems. Dr William Gunn, of Glasgow's Public Health Department, had to admit in 1929, that despite much demolition since 1925, there were still 13,568 condemned houses, with an estimated population of c. 37,000 over the age of fifteen. About 26 per cent of the original slum dwellers had not accepted the opportunity of getting into one of the new houses. You

cannot change people by Act of Parliament...
There were strong social and financial reasons
for customer resistance to a change in housing.
In the uncertainties of life, some were reluctant
to leave the support of a known set of
neighbours if they came from a bad close with
good people living in it, whom they could rely
on to help in cases of emergency. The extended
family was also an inhibiting factor in moving
off into the unknown. If a family had spent a
generation manoeuvring and manipulating with
the people who factored the houses, so that they
could be near one another, and have granny
handy, it seemed a pity to move away. Rent
arrears also increased worry about debt. For
example, in the Germiston district of Glasgow
in 1936, out of 492 houses that were occupied,
140 tenants left, and 105 of them were in arrears
with rent. Dr Gunn reported that about 20 per
cent of families in the Calton area preferred to
remain in their slum dwellings, and about 10
per cent returned to their old district after being
re-housed. Paying the rent provided the worst
headache for those on low-income budgets,
where it assumed a larger share the poorer the
household. Scotland always had a higher
incidence of landlord-tenant problems than
England. For example, around 1890 London had
one eviction per 1,800 inhabitants, to Glasgow's

one eviction per 55 inhabitants. Relationships between tenant and factor were the stuff of Glasgow's music-hall comics. For example: a Factor who was called out to a tenement flat to investigate a complaint about dry rot, passes a mouse trap with a trout in it in the lobby, and asks the tenant 'Why is that trout in the mouse trap?' Tenant says, 'We'll talk about the dampness later!'

At the bottom end of the scale, Glasgow had attempted to alleviate the problem of housing the homeless, by building seven 'model' lodging houses between 1871 and 1884. The 'models', as they came to be called by Glaswegians, were used by the homeless for temporary stopovers. The smallest, in Greendyke Street, had 266 beds, and the largest, in Portugal Street in the Gorbals, had 437 beds. The lodgers lived under the supervision of superintendents, who were usually ex-military men of the 'nemo me impune lacessit' ('who dares meddle with me?') variety, able to look after themselves in any physical encounters. Lodgers paid 3d or 4½d a night for a cubicle separated from the others by seven-foot high partitions. Each cubicle had a comfortable bed. Bedclothes were aired daily and changed weekly. The popularity and overcrowding of the 'models' resulted in an overflow of people in from the cold, who opted for "a tuppeny hing". They were allowed to sleep sitting on the floor of the hallway or lobby of the model lodging-house, alternating single arms over a clothes rope slung from one end to the other, fastened to a hook, and 'hing' or hang out there for the night. Residents had to be out of the sleeping area by 8 am. The 'lobby dossers' were later to become enshrined in the name of the sheriff of Calton Creek, Lobey Dosser, in Bud Neill's cartoon strip for the Glasgow *Evening Times*. They were roused in the mornings in the 'models' by the simple expedient of the Superintendent untying the clothes rope! Residents in the 'models' had the use of the other parts of the building twenty-four hours a day, including a kitchen with hotplate, cooking utensils and dishes, a roomy dining hall and recreation rooms. A shop sold uncooked food and there was bath and lavatory accommodation. Free Bibles were available and regular religious services were held. Educational lectures were given aimed at improving skills, manners and morals. It was all included as part of the regular timetable. The Glasgow Police kept a watching brief on the 'models', especially at weekends.

What kind of people came into the 'models'? Bell and Paton attempted a profile in 1896. 'They are of all nationalities...disrobed

Jock Troup - *on Naval Patrol*

Peter Connoly - *before and after BTI!*

Wedding Day
*Jock Troup and Katie Black
married in Inverness 1928*

Troup Family Photo
*Jock, Betty (1931), Rona (1929),
Ian (1933) and Katie*

Jimmy Byres - *before and after conversion*

Open-air Preaching
A lunchtime crowd

'Supper for Servicemen'

Tent Hall Program
Christmas and New Year 1941-42

Tent Hall Service 1950s

Jock Troup
in a Pensive Mood

clergymen and street bullies, decayed gentlemen and area sneaks, tramps and tinkers, labourers, sweeps, thieves and thimble-riggers (thimble-rig is a betting game). The moral tone is low, the habits are generally unclean, and so sometimes is the language'. A good number of these folk found their way to the Free Breakfast for the Poor at the Tent Hall each Sunday morning. Queuing generally began to form around the Tent Hall in Steel Street from about 5 am, and the Free Breakfast for the Poor generally fed about 1,200 people every Sunday. The Poor Children's Sabbath Dinner catered for about 700 every Sunday.

Jock Troup had an established reputation as a preacher and evangelist at the Tent Hall. The Tent Hall Sub-Committee minute of 1 February 1932 reports: 'In the absence of Mr McRostie through illness, a special Gospel Campaign begins on Sunday 14 February, conducted by Evangelist Jock Troup, whose messages are powerful and fruitful, and whose services are much appreciated by the people'.

The Tent Hall Sub-Committee minute of 4 April 1932 stated: 'Evangelist Jock Troup had been with them for some weeks, and compared with ordinary weeks the attendance had been exceedingly good, between 500 and 600 on week nights and over 1,000 on Sabbath nights. There had been some good cases dealt with.....Many of these continued to do well, and had become helpers at the open air meetings'.

Towards the end of 1932, Peter McRostie's health was failing and there was a Glasgow United Evangelistic Association meeting called so that its Committee of Management could consider appointing someone to act as Assistant Superintendent of the Tent Hall. The minute of that meeting states: 'The name of Mr Jock Troup having been recommended as being the most suitable person for the work, it was agreed to appoint a small committee with powers, consisting of the following gentlemen: Lord Maclay, Messrs Allan Arthur, Hugh Brown and R.B. Stewart'.

On 1 September 1932, Sandy Galbraith wrote to Jock on behalf of the GUEA Directors to arrange a meeting prior to the formal meeting at midday on the following Monday. On 14 November 1932, Mr Allan Arthur submitted a minute of the special committee of 13 September 1932, in connection with the appointment of Mr J. Troup as Assistant Superintendent.

There was a Welcome Social in Glasgow for Jock Troup on 26 October 1932, at 7.30 pm. The tea ticket cost 4d. To illustrate the social problems of the period, on 30 October, hunger marchers converged on London, and there was a 15,000-strong rally in Trafalgar Square against means tests and mass unemployment. The police clashed with the jobless, and fought with youths for hours. Fifty were injured and fourteen people were arrested. To confirm that the ugly mood of the Depression years was not confined to London, on 22 December 1932, fifteen people were injured in Glasgow when the police clashed with the jobless there, and a policeman was thrown into the River Clyde. Jock was not coming to work in 'Easy Street'!

How did Glasgow and the Tent Hall respond to Jock Troup, as the 'new kid on the block' in 1932? Remember, he was well known to the Glaswegians as a visiting preacher and there was great joy at his arrival to work full-time as P.T. McRostie's assistant. He had a track record as a colourful character ever since his time spent as a BTI student and Glaswegians, colourful characters themselves, revelled in this. I have an unsolicited account, written by an ex-BTI student, W.B. Forsyth, from Leamington Spa, who gives his first impression of Jock Troup preaching at the Tent Hall (October 1925) in the following terms:

> On the first or second Saturday night in Glasgow I was taken to the Tent Hall. That was a cultural shock: the unadorned building, a congregation of close to a thousand, all

working-class, and with a good number of the 'flotsam and jetsam' swept in from Glasgow Green. In my young care-free days, we called them, with pitying contempt, 'the great unwashed'. Young fools we were! That night I sat with them and became one with them.

Right on time the platform party filed in, led by Peter McRostie, the Superintendent, and including the preacher Jock Troup. We bellowed forth Sankey's hymns and C.S.S.M. choruses as an introductory, softening-up process. The notices followed, and it was the signal for pandemonium to break loose. Protestors rose and began to heckle McRostie. 'Last Saturday you ordered a soul for whom Christ died to be manhandled and flung out of the hall' etc., etc. McRostie did not say a word. He looked at his opponents and one felt the Spirit-filled power of his personality targeting one after the other. His look silenced them. They were deflated. Only then did he give a short crisp explanation. The man was drunk and disorderly, shouting out and disrupting the meeting, preventing others from hearing the Gospel of saving grace. The stewards could not calm him down, the only place for him was 'outer darkness'. The notices then continued: 'Tomorrow, Sabbath forenoon at 8 o'clock the Men's Breakfast, followed by Gospel preaching....Sabbath midday, the children's dinner...'

McRostie faded into the background and Jock Troup took over. It was a lantern-lecture – Bible stories depicted on three-inch hand-coloured glass slides. With his introductory remarks he captured the attention of his audience, and then, the lights were dimmed, and he delivered his message. His voice was loud and penetrating: his speech betrayed his Scottish origins. He spoke the language of the people, language they easily understood: the Gospel delivered in a straight-from-the-shoulder way, but with unction and power and persuasion. It was obvious that the Spirit of God was at work. The lights went up and Jock, who had been fully clothed when the lights were dimmed, had, during the message, flung off his jacket and waistcoat, his collar and tie, and he was standing in his shirtsleeves, trousers and braces. His face glistened with sweat. His whole being, mind, body and soul, had been freely given to get the message across. And, he succeeded. Souls were saved that night.

I had seen strange things that night. I had heard the Gospel preached to the poor. My own mission was under way. In Brazil, I spent a missionary career preaching mainly to the poor, but I was no Jock Troup!

The Tent Hall Sub-Committee minute of 9 January 1933 reports that Mr Troup was getting on well, and was much liked.

In April 1933, the Troup family joy was complete when their little son Ian was born in the new home in Giffnock, Glasgow.

The Finance Sub-Committee of 26 June 1933 reported that Mr McRostie had booked his passage to South Africa, sailing on 17 September 1933, and that his resignation from the Tent Hall might be expected shortly. In view of the valuable services rendered to the work of the Association over a long period of years, it was agreed to grant him a retiring allowance of £150 per annum from the date when resignation should take effect, probably 1 September 1933.

The GUEA Committee of 4 September 1933 reported on Mr McRostie's death, and recorded the following tribute:

By the death of Mr P.T. McRostie, the Directors of the GUEA have lost a beloved colleague and servant, and the City of Glasgow one who laboured long and earnestly for the moral and spiritual welfare of her people in the working-class and poorer districts of the City. Endowed with marked Scriptural gifts and upheld by a physical fitness which never seemed to tire, Mr McRostie filled a unique place in the evangelical life of the City. As Superintendent for seven years at Bethany Hall and afterwards for over twenty-five years at the Tent Hall, he acted as a guide and counsellor and friend to the poor and needy, and was instrumental in turning many to righteousness. A man of lovable and generous disposition, he was held in high esteem by all sections of the community. Many will look back with grateful remembrance on the history of the work accomplished for the kingdom of God by this devoted servant of Christ. In recording their respect for his memory, and their appreciation of the valuable service rendered by him, the Directors also beg to assure Mrs McRostie and the family circle of their earnest prayer that God will multiply to them the comforts of His grace, and make their hearts sanctuaries of His peace...

On the recommendation of the Tent Hall Sub-Committee of this date, it was agreed to appoint Mr J. Troup as Superintendent in charge of the work of the Tent Hall and that his salary be increased from £300 to £350 as from 1 November 1933.

The Finance Sub-Committee report of 11 September 1933 says, under the heading 'Grant to Mrs McRostie': 'In view of the high esteem in which the late Mr McRostie is held, it was resolved to make a voluntary grant to his widow, of £150 and also three voluntary grants of £52 payable at the pleasure of the Directors over the next few years.'

Peter McRostie had been an outstanding Superintendent. How would Jock Troup shape up to the increased responsibility? Jock was a 'people person' who threw himself wholeheartedly into this work. Bert Clark, a Tent Hall worker, remembered Jock as what he called 'a man's man', always manly, and respected by men. Bob Clapham commented on the high percentage of men who stood listening at the Glasgow Cross open-air meetings. Young men admired him, older men deferred to him. He was always well-dressed and hearty, totally self-giving in the work to which God called him. The Glasgow people loved him, and responded to him warmly. He was very direct in his manner, but never a bully. He would prefer to invite people to join him in a piece of work rather than order them to do so. If he met a well-off Christian, he would never shrink from telling them how worthwhile a current project was, and ask them to support it. Jock was completely at ease with people like Lord Maclay. In fact, Lord Maclay would regularly get his chauffeur up early on a Sunday morning, and be driven into the city so that he could attend the Free Breakfast for the Poor, and hear Jock preaching. He called Jock 'my prodigal son' because, he said, Jock was 'always coming to the father for money!' One lady said that Jock Troup could have gone into any shop in the Saltmarket area around the Tent Hall, and asked for anything, and the shopkeepers would have given it to him! His family told how he sometimes came home minus his overcoat because he had met someone who needed it. He often came home late at night with empty pockets because he had been talking to someone in need.

The GUEA Minute of 8 January 1934 gave a progress report:

Mr Troup gave a brief account of the special New Year meetings. Rt Hon. Lord Provost A.B. Swan occupied the chair at the Hogmanay Supper, where over 1,600 of the needy poor were provided with a warm and nourishing meal, and heard messages of Gospel hope and cheer.

They began the New Year with a special Gospel Campaign conducted by Rev. H.A. Morrison of Belfast accompanied by the Spiritual Jubilee Singing Quintette.

GUEA Minute of 5 March 1934 reports: Mr Troup stated that the recent Gospel Campaign had been the means of bringing scores of new people about the Tent Hall. Over a hundred decisions for Christ had been recorded and altogether the work and the workers were in a healthy spiritual condition. Some of J.W. Meiklejohn's children's meetings had an attendance of 700.   J.W. Meiklejohn had graduated Master of Arts from Glasgow University, and had joined the GUEA staff after a session at BTI He and P.W. Petty of Scripture Union organized camps and missions during the summer months. J.W. Meiklejohn, later known to generations of Scripture Union campers as 'Boss', did a great work for God during his time on the GUEA staff. He conducted nine children's missions during the winter of 1933–34. The Bible Class had 110 young men and women attending regularly at the beginning of 1935. J.W. Meiklejohn's salary was increased from £150 to £180 from 1 January 1935.

Like those around him, Jock gave himself unstintingly to the work of the Lord in the Tent Hall. During the week, he often went out to speak at open-air meetings at the works gates of the shipyards, like Fairfields in Govan, Barclay Curle's yard, and John Brown of Clydebank. Huge crowds gathered to hear the revivalist preacher, and there were people who came to Christ at these meetings.

One of them was a self-confessed ballroom dancing fanatic, Arthur Campbell, who later became a youth leader and Missions Treasurer at the Tent Hall and Pastor of Hermon Baptist Church in Glasgow. Bob Clapham, as a young man in his dungarees, remembers hearing Jock preaching at Fairfields' gate during the lunch-break. The Communists were strong in these difficult years. Bob Clapham recalls a big man with a Communist sign on his lapel, grumbling and moaning at the opposite side of the ring while Jock was speaking. Jock went right over, and stood in front of the man, and spoke in a LOUD voice :'Get in that shipyard, or apart from the grace of God, some of us won't be able to keep our hands in our pockets!' The man beat a hasty retreat...

Notorious drunkards like Jimmy Byres (see photo section) were totally transformed by the Gospel of God's grace.

Raymond McKeown was another young man who came to Christ through the ministry of Jock Troup in the open-air meetings at Glasgow Cross. The McKeown family had moved into the Gorbals district of Glasgow (via Kirkintilloch) when they came over from Ulster in the 1930s. Raymond's dad Joseph was an ex-Army man who had served in the Royal Ulster Constabulary, but when his wife Margaret became a target and had been shot at, they decided to move to Scotland.

Mother Margaret came into an experience of salvation through the ministry of the Tent Hall, and Joseph, Eileen and Ruth followed soon afterwards. Raymond was the loose cannon, the rebel in the family. Raymond had been granted his wish as he grew up to absent himself from the Tent Hall gatherings, with the exception of the weekly Bible class conducted by R.C. Brown who was not the kind of man you went up to and slapped on the back. The author remembers him when he was an old man. He was very smartly dressed in a smart dark-blue pinstripe suit, and his shirt had a starched, 'fly-away' collar. No words were wasted, and every word was weighed. He liked to outline his talks on a blackboard, and even as an elderly man, amazed the onlooker by writing, with chalk, in brilliant copperplate style. R.C. Brown was a key Tent Hall worker, greatly respected for his godliness and practical wisdom. I have no doubt that his influence, among others like George Bell and Willie Brown, was felt by Raymond.

Raymond was a gifted singer, footballer and soapbox orator. He had adopted a strident, anarchic interest in things atheistic, and became a voracious reader of Paine, Darwin, Huxley, and the *Free Thinker* newspaper. He competed with the noisy trams and the late shoppers in Glasgow's equivalent of Hyde Park Corner – Brunswick Street off Argyle Street – on Saturday evenings, sharing his learning as a soapbox orator. Seventeen-year-olds have (or think they have) amazing insights way beyond their years...

It was the era of the open-air meeting, and Jock Troup, Superintendent of the Tent Hall was a master. Hundreds attended his open air meetings at Glasgow Cross, and on one occasion Raymond found himself among the crowd. Moved by what he heard at the meeting, Raymond later found his way into the evening meeting, and sitting in the upstairs section, he could see his two sisters in the choir, and his parents in the lower area of the hall. When Jock Troup ended his message and went into his normal impassioned appeal for people to make known their need of Christ, Raymond the young rebel went to the side room and was helped by a converted alcoholic to find Christ as his own Lord and Saviour. Raymond became a strong leader in Christian work, and cut his teeth as a preacher and singer in the back-court open-air meetings run by Tent Hall workers. He became a great open air speaker, leading a regular meeting at Glasgow's famous 'Barras', a street market and gathering-place for hooks, crooks and comic singers. Raymond added lots of grace and spice to his meetings by his treatment of hecklers.

If Jock was king of the open-air meeting, Raymond later became heir-apparent.

When Jock was speaking at the open-air meeting at Glasgow Cross, he was being troubled once by a heckler, who finally announced that he was fed up listening to Jock going on about 'the outpoured wrath of God', and instead would be going into the local pub. The story goes that the man asked the barman for a pint of the outpoured wrath of God – and **then dropped dead**. We have no record of what happened next.

There is another story of Jock at work in the open air, which demonstrates his knowledge of human nature. Jock had been on holiday, and while he was away the young people had been troubled by a man who had been brought up in the Jewish faith, and knew his Old Testament well enough to give the young people a hard time with his heckling. When they complained to Jock on his return from holiday, he told them he would come to the meeting, but he would stand at the fringe and they should carry on with their usual procedures. When their troublesome friend started giving them bother, Jock stepped into the ring and pointed to the man. 'If you don't leave these young people alone and go away now, I'm going to tell everyone here everything I know about you!' The man left in a hurry. After the meeting, someone asked Jock what he knew about the man, to which he replied: 'I knew he had a conscience!'

The variety of versions of Jock's dealing with a drunken heckler in the Tent Hall reveals that perhaps this kind of thing happened a number of times during Jock's twelve years at the Tent. He supposedly threw out a drunk for disruptive behaviour. I tend to agree with those who have told me Jock would never use physical violence. What I know of his physique and voice and Christian grace makes me agree with them. At any rate, someone is reported as remonstrating with Jock for ejecting the man, in the following terms: 'Jesus would never have done that. He would have cast the demon out of the man.' Jock replied: 'Well, first of all, I'm not Jesus. And secondly, I knew when I put the man out, I put the demon out as well!'

I have had an eyewitness report of Jock at an open-air meeting in Inverness, when a young soldier who was the worse for drink, was being objectionable. Jock excused himself and took the young soldier away quietly. He brought him back shortly afterwards and reported that the young man had something to tell the crowd. Jock had just led him to Christ and this was his first attempt to give testimony to his new-found faith.

During his time at the Tent Hall, Jock formed a friendship with one of Ulster's best-known evangelists, William Patteson (W.P.)

Nicholson. He was God's man for the hour in the powder-keg that was Ulster in the 1920s. Some of his critics called him 'The Vulgar Evangelist' because he spoke in the language of the working classes. Dr Ian Paisley writes: 'To say he was unique is to be guilty of colossal understatement'. Hundreds of Belfast shipyard workers marched from their yards to churches in the city where his Missions were being held. W.P. had a Christian heritage – his middle name Patteson was given in gratitude for the ministry of Rev. W. Patteson of Bangor, the family's home town.

After a wild and wicked lifestyle as a merchant seaman, and later working on the construction of the Cape-to-Cairo railway in South Africa, he was saved sitting in the chair at home, reading the newspaper and smoking while his mother was preparing the breakfast. It was 8.30 am on Monday 22 May 1899. God had been speaking for some time through storms at sea and through crisis circumstances. He had returned home, and from that morning, as he put it, 'I became a new creature and began hating sin'. He had a subsequent experience of total yielding to the Holy Spirit after hearing a message by Rev. J. Stuart Holden at a Convention for the Deepening of Spiritual Life.

At the age of 26, he did what Jock Troup was

to do later. He became a student at the Bible Training Institute, Glasgow, in December 1901. He was ordained as an evangelist of the Presbyterian Church in Carlisle in 1914. Like Jock Troup, he had seen what could only be described as revival blessing in Lanarkshire, Scotland, and in Ulster – Bangor and Portadown, Lurgan and Newtonards, Lisburn and Belfast. When he preached restitution in Belfast as a valid component of true repentance, Harland and Wolff, the shipbuilding yard, had to build sheds to contain the stolen goods that were returned!

He had made many visits to Scotland, notably some missioning in Lanarkshire in 1903, and a year substituting for Pastor D.J. Findlay of the Tabernacle, St George's Cross, Glasgow, who had gone to Australia to recover from a breakdown. Perhaps we could relate one incident which would illustrate how a man like W.P. Nicholson could become a 'bosom buddy' of a man like Jock Troup. When Nicholson was taking a tent mission in Lanarkshire, a big strong miner came to help, and held the wooden tent-pegs, while the evangelist in dungarees and vest, was swinging a fourteen-pound hammer, sweating profusely in the summer sunshine. The miner spent a lot of time denigrating the preacher, predicting that he would come – fat, lazy, well-dressed, and useless – 'after you have done all the hard work.' The evangelist said nothing. Stanley Barnes wrote:

> The first meeting was held the next Sunday afternoon, and when William reached the platform, who should he see but the big miner. The man looked up at him in amazement; evidently, he could not believe that the evangelist was the same hard-working fellow who the other day had been soaked in sweat with the effort of swinging a fourteen-pound hammer. When giving the announcements and introducing himself, William said 'I have something good to tell you about the erecting of the tent'. He then related the story of the big miner who had helped him. He spared not a word as he described that afternoon's activities and the cynical comments made about the preacher. He ended his story by disclosing that the miner was there in the tent. William did not name him, or point him out, but most of the audience knew him to be a notable sinner, and had a good laugh. The big miner did not seem to mind, and by the end of the service he had accepted Christ as Saviour.

Later in his life, W.P. made several visits to the Tent Hall, and became a staunch friend and

partner in the Gospel for Jock Troup.
He wrote to encourage Jock in October 1936 :

> My Dear Brother Troup,
> So glad the good work is going on in the Hall
> – sinners getting converted. There is no work
> like it anywhere. How often I visit you when
> I have His ear, and also dear brother Galbraith
> at the Bethel. Though sundered far, we meet
> around the common mercy seat. Hallelujah!
> Many thanks for inviting us over there. I
> won't forget, and the Tent Hall would be like
> coming home...ask those good prayer partners
> in the Hall to pray hard for us over here. We
> can't do without their love and their
> prayers...I have an Austin saloon. A beauty.
> Have you any golf over there? What about
> Tuesdays? I haven't had a game since landing
> here. Wow! Wow! Are you coming over?
> I'll hug you half to death if you come. Keep
> believing. Remember us to our mutual
> friends. Keep your pecker up and a good stiff
> upper lip. Never wilt or compromise. Love
> me and pray for me.
>   Yours as Ever for Ever,
>   Wm P. Nicholson.

7

Tent Hall Days – A Cameo of Faith

Perhaps we should make a few explanatory comments about the Superintendent's role at the Tent Hall. He was there to see that the affairs of the Hall ran smoothly, but there were people who attended to the nuts and bolts of the daily ministry. The Superintendent was involved at the sharp end of the pastoral needs of the people who came around the Hall, as well as caring for its regular workers. The Tent Hall was in many ways the ordinary people's church in the district, but a good number of those who attended were communicant members of the Church of Scotland, who made their contribution to the Tent Hall work as an additional piece of Christian service. During Jock Troup's superintendency, he often spoke at the Free Breakfast for the Poor and the Poor Children's Sabbath Dinner, where he preached Gospel addresses. He was speaking to some people who were hungry for food, and some people who were hungry for God, but he was not regularly involved in Saturday and Sunday ministry. As far as the Christian public in Glasgow were concerned, and this extended to the author's time, the Tent Hall had a particular place in the affections of Christians. Glasgow in the thirties was a very busy place as far as things evangelical were concerned. The Saturday edition of the Glasgow *Evening Citizen* contained two pages of church notices, with additional articles by their special reporter 'Churchman'.

During the summer months, it was the pattern that when the winter programme of Saturday evening meetings in their home church was over, people attended the Tent Hall on Saturdays. For courting couples (only the names have been suppressed to protect the innocent!) it was a cheap night out with your girl-friend or boy-friend, in a wholesome Christian atmosphere. The Superintendent acted as Chairman of the Saturday Evening Rallies, and a wide variety of preachers and musicians were invited along. Here is a selection of what was on offer at the Tent Hall on Saturday evenings in the 1930s, with some news of counter-attractions in the city: There were regular musical items by the Tent Hall Senior Choir, Junior Choir and Orchestra. On 24 December 1932, the week after Meiklejohn and McPhail returned to the Rangers team, after injury, the Saturday Rally at the Tent Hall featured the Motherwell Hallelujah Hall Gospel Band.

On 16 January 1933 you could visit Carl Hagenbeck's Wonder Zoo at the Kelvin Hall Carnival and on 21 January attend Special Gospel Campaign meetings with Mr and Mrs Seth Sykes. Seth Sykes had worked on Glasgow's trams, and had volunteered at the outbreak of World War I to become a soldier in what became known as 'The Tramway Battalion'. After the War, through the encouragement of John McIlveen of Lambhill Mission, the couple became evangelists specializing in Gospel work among children. They had their send-off into full-time work from the Orphan Hall, James Morrison Street, Glasgow. Seth's wife Bessie was a gifted musician, a prolific writer of hymns and choruses which she sang, playing a small pedal, harmonium. Her best-known compositions were 'Thank You Lord, for Saving my Soul' and 'Love, Wonderful Love'. On 4 March 1933 the Glasgow public could see the film *Million Dollar Legs* starring Jack Oakie, Andy Clyde and Susan Fleming, or they could attend the Tent Hall's celebration of P.T. McRostie's Semi-Jubilee. On 30 March 1934 there was a Special Lantern Lecture (these were a fairly regular feature, covering subjects like 'The Pilgrim Fathers', 'Pilgrim's Progress', 'The Sinking of the Titanic', and 'The Fresh-Air Fortnight'). On this occasion the subject was 'The Wandering Jew' presented by Rev. Armin A. Holzer Th.B, Ph.D., who would speak over the weekend on 'St John's Patmos Vision', 'The Lord's Second Advent' and 'The Battle of Armageddon – the Coming Great World War'. Through the week there was also a series of addresses on 'The Tabernacle in the Wilderness' or 'The Gospel According to Moses'. The soloist on 30 March was W. Simpson Moor ('pupil of Signor Victorio Ricci, the Great Italian Master'.) On 6 October 1934 there was a Lantern Lecture by Arthur P. Smith on 'The Work of God among Post Office Officials in China'. On 22 December 1934 people could hear The Savoy Boys' Quintette, and on 29 December 1934, Rev. Herbert Lockyer gave a Lantern Lecture of 'The Life of Mary Slessor' – advertized as 'illustrated with the finest set of slides in the country'. Herbert Lockyer and Peter Connolly spoke at the 'Grand New Year Soiree' on 1 January 1935, and there was the commencement of a Special Mission by Captain Reginald Wallis. There were regular 'Deputations' with groups from the Christian Police Association, The Christian Nurses, the

Postal Workers' Christian Fellowship, and the Bible Training Institute students. On 19 January 1935 the 'Coloured Quintette of Jubilee Singers' from Cleveland, Ohio, were featured, with Rev. James Emblem. Rev. Peter Donald said they introduced themselves in the following manner: 'We are a Christian Organization, saved from condemnation through old-fashioned salvation. We have made our consecration, and have the blessing of sanctification. We sing with inspiration without hesitation to any congregation, colour, race or nation, providing their qualification meets with God's approbation, and we trust God for our remuneration!'

The guest preacher on 9 February was Evan Jones, 'the Welsh Singing Evangelist', and on 16 February there was a Lantern Lecture on 'Mission Work in Amazonia'. On 16 March 1935 Glasgow people could hear the Edinburgh Excelsior Singers or go to the cinema to see Ronald Coleman in *Bulldog Drummond Strikes Back*. Rev. John McKendrick preached occasionally, and the Russell Brothers – Jimmy, Tom and Ralph – from Kirkintilloch, came singing occasionally. Rev. Austen Stirling, well-known for his concept of the Gospel as a 'Red-Hot Snowball' also spoke occasionally. On Saturday 15 August 1936, Evangelist Tom

Paterson spoke. (He and John Thomson used to go with Jock Troup on his shipyard open-air meetings. He became known later in Independent Evangelical circles as 'McBeth Paterson'.)

As a minor social comment we might note that the Women's League of Health and Beauty hit the headlines on 11 June 1937. They apologized to the BBC for some Canadian girls, in Britain for the Festival of Beauty at Wembley, who had gone into the Alexandra Palace restaurant *bare-legged* because they were waiting for a rehearsal. This kind of thing would not happen again!

Sometimes, top Bible teachers were invited to the Tent Hall. On Saturday 12 August 1939 Dr Donald Gray Barnhouse of Philadelphia, USA, began a series of studies on the Book of Revelation ('Don't Miss Hearing These Wonderful Messages'). His sermon title for Sunday at 7 pm was 'An Audience That Wanted to Murder the Preacher'. (Mmm...sounds interesting!) Jock was utterly loyal and supportive of his employers, and helped to fund-raise for Tent Hall projects. He was scrupulously honest with finance. R.C. Brown, GUEA Secretary, wrote to him regarding the reseating of the Tent Hall, on 11 November 1937:

I am happy to acknowledge your cheque for £100 which with your previous payments, makes a grand total of Four Hundred and Eighty-eight pounds, Nineteen shillings and tenpence sterling (£488.19.10d). My Directors have expressed to you on more than one occasion, their gratitude and appreciation of the efforts you have made to raise this handsome sum. They desire me to express to the workers and friends who have contributed to the reseating of the Tent Hall, their sincere thanks for the loyal support and co-operation shown in making the house of the Lord beautiful.   They rejoice with you in the completion of the task you have set yourself, and pray the blessing of God in still more abundant measure may rest on the work and the workers.

Yours sincerely, R.C. Brown.

During the month of September 1938, by an amazing venture of faith, Jock Troup made it possible for very large numbers of people in Glasgow to hear the great American Pastor, Dr Harry Ironside, of Moody Memorial Church, Chicago. The Tent Hall took over Green's Playhouse Cinema for the Sunday afternoons and evenings of the month of September, with a Special Mission to coincide with Glasgow's smash-hit Empire Exhibition at Bellahouston Park. In September 1938 the 80,000-ton liner

Queen Elizabeth was launched from John Brown's shipyard on the Clyde.

The Playhouse complex contained a cinema, a ballroom, offices, tearooms and a putting range. The cinema was the biggest covered auditorium in Europe at that time, and it was built through the entrepreneurial skills of the Green family. The Greens (father George and sons Fred and Bert) were legendary in the history of Glasgow entertainment. They were a Lancashire family of show-people who had moved their circus show from Wigan to Glasgow, and performed at the show-ground on the former site of Gallowgate Barracks in Glasgow's East End. In 1896, the first year motion pictures were shown in London, George Green went to Friese-Green and Paul in London to buy a projector and camera equipment. They were soon showing motion pictures to the public, at the show-ground, in a booth measuring 50 feet by 30 feet, into which they could just fit 500 standing customers, who paid one penny each for admission. Glaswegians are inveterately curious and trendy people, so the early shows were a great success. This inspired George Green to have an ornate, collapsible 800-seat booth made, at a cost of £8,000, and soon they were having travelling 'Kinema' shows. From March 1911 onwards, there were a series of 'Picturedromes', starting from the Gorbals. The great leap forward took place in 1922, the year after the revival in East Anglia. George Green and his sons sent the architect John Fairweather to America to familiarize himself with the latest trends in cinema design. Bruce Peter writes:

> The trip resulted, after four years of construction, in a 4,368-seat mammoth cinema stretching from Renfield Street to West Nile Street. Green's Playhouse was a triumph of careful planning. The ballroom had a reputed maximum capacity of 6,000 dancers. The whole project was gigantic, involving forty-five companies, requiring 16,000 tons of cement, and needing special girders and trusses to be designed to support the double-tiered cinema auditorium and the ballroom above it. George Singleton commented: 'For private individuals to invest so heavily in such a marvellous project, way before the advent of "talkies" must have taken great courage indeed. I have always admired the Greens for their boldness; their Glasgow Playhouse was a most remarkable theatre.'

George Green's two sons, Fred and Bert, supervized the work. They were very astute businessmen. They used home-grown labour as far as possible in the building work. Clowns, acrobats and showmen, usually employed elsewhere in the company, were given training in plumbing, joinery and bricklaying skills, and were set to work. The job was so carefully costed that, to save on travel costs, the workers walked every day from the Gallowgate showground to the Renfield Street site, and many outside contractors faced financially punitive penalties for delayed or unsatisfactory work.

The cinema was opened with great public acclaim and interest by Mrs Mason, the Lady Provost of Glasgow, on 15 September 1927, with Monty Banks in *Play Safe* as the main feature. The marquee-type canopy, the big advertising signs, and the enormous vertical name sign, lit in the American style by hundreds of bulbs, with the 'U' of 'PLAYHOUSE' mounted crookedly to echo the Greens' advertising slogan 'We Want U In' was for decades a spectacular eye-catcher at the top of Renfield Street. There were massive staircases and lifts to the auditorium, with its huge Corinthian columns along the side walls, interspersed with boxes. The design was heavy neo-classical, with very bright orange, primrose and gold colour schemes. The eye-catching murals were designed by John Alexander, a Newcastle-based interior decorator, famous for his rich cinema creations. There was a colour change lighting system and the seats were colour-coded according to the price of the tickets. Luxury double seats, known as 'Golden Divans', were marketed as just the job for courting couples. In the era of the silent movies, an orchestra accompanied the show and the high-kicking Playhouse dancers performed their risqué routines every weekend as part of the lavish entertainment.

We can imagine that there was a certain customer resistance on the part of the dour and staid Directors of the Tent Hall, when Jock Troup suggested leaving the Tent Hall and taking over Greens Playhouse for a few Sundays. Jock felt that the Tent Hall couldn't hold the crowds of Glaswegians who would want to hear Dr Harry Ironside. Jock knew his man, for Jock had been Scotland's representative at the Moody Centenary in Chicago and other cities in America in 1937. He had met Harry Ironside, and knew that he was the kind of colourful character Glaswegians would respond to. Some of the Tent Hall Directors were reluctant to move to what they might regard as a den of iniquity. Some were worried about the financing of the enterprise, for the cost was to be £300 a day, a lot of money in the thirties. Jock tried to smooth the ruffled feathers, and, to the Directors' credit, it happened! They moved from the 2,400-seat Tent Hall to the 4,368-seat Playhouse. The Special Mission of September 1938 was timed to coincide with the Empire Exhibition in Bellahouston Park Glasgow. The Glasgow *Evening Citizen* reported that 'Green's Playhouse has been secured for Sunday services during the month of September, at 3.30 and 8 pm.' In Scotland, there was (and still is!) a well-loved confectionery item called 'Highland Toffee', with a drawing of a Highland cow on the front. The Cowans who marketed this product, were a Christian Brethren family, and they gave the whole thing a good kick-start by funding the first Sunday. The *Evening Citizen* of 10 September urged the readers: 'Don't miss hearing America's greatest Gospel Preacher and Bible Teacher, and also America's finest Gospel Singer'.

Harry Ironside's grandparents had emigrated to Canada from New Deer, Aberdeenshire. Harry's dad John married Sophia Stafford, a Methodist Church choir member, when he was twenty-three. They settled in Toronto, where John worked as a teller in the Merchants Bank and became very active as a street preacher with the Christian Brethren. John was nicknamed 'The Eternity Man' because he was constantly

asking people, 'Where will you spend eternity?'
Little Harry was born in Canada in October
1876. When Harry was born, he was reckoned
to be dead, but the nurse in attendance found a
pulse forty minutes after the doctor had set the
baby aside as lifeless in order to attend to the
mother, who was very ill. The nurse plunged
the baby into a hot bath, he yelled, and thus a
preacher was born. The Eternity Man died of
typhoid fever aged twenty-six, three weeks after
his second son John was born, when Harry was
about two years old. The family moved from
Canada to America (Los Angeles, California)
in 1886. Sophia had a hard struggle raising her
boys by using her sewing skills to make coats
and garments which she sold. She was a godly
woman, and a keen personal witness, who led
many of her customers to Christ in her home.
Harry started memorizing Scripture from the
time he was three years old. From the age of
eight, he claimed to read through the whole
Bible at least once a year, and by the age of
fourteen he said he had 'caught up with himself',
that is, he had read the Bible right through
fourteen times. He continued to do that until
1948, when cataracts prevented him. This means
that he read the Bible right through at least
seventy-two times! Billy Graham said that
Ironside knew the Bible better than anyone he

had ever met. Before he had a personal experience of Christ as his Saviour, he ran a neighbourhood Sunday School, when he was twelve years old, with about sixty regular attenders. He was greatly impressed by D.L. Moody's preaching in Hazzard Pavilion, Los Angeles. Perched on a trough-like girder far above the congregation of 8,000, Harry heard Moody preach on Daniel 5:27 'Thou art weighed in the balances, and found wanting'. He was converted to Christ soon after at the age of fourteen, and began preaching immediately. His only formal education beyond grammar school was in the Salvation Army's San Diego Cadet School, and Oakland Training Garrison, from which he passed out as a lieutenant aged sixteen. When he left his work at the Lamson Photo Studios, his boss said, 'a good photographer has been spoiled to make a poor preacher'.

He became known as 'The Boy Preacher of Los Angeles', and stayed with the Salvation Army until he joined the Plymouth Brethren in 1896. Harry Ironside spent two months each summer for at least twelve years, ministering among the Native Americans of the South-West, in Arizona and New Mexico. From 1924 onwards, he held many meetings under the direction of the Moody Bible Institute, and was visiting professor at Dallas Theological

Seminary from 1925 until 1943. His only pastorate was at Moody Memorial Church, Chicago, from 1930 until 1948. He wrote over sixty books. His commentaries are written in a clear, practical style. Dr Harry A. Ironside brought a fine soloist with him to Scotland. Stratton Shufelt was minister of music at Moody Memorial Church, and served as soloist and song leader in the Special Mission. His wife was his accompanist. Stratton Shufelt was well known for his rendition of 'The Ninety and Nine'. He returned to Britain later, after the First World War, with the youthful Billy Graham and Chuck Templeton. Harry Ironside's visit to Glasgow in 1938 at the behest of Jock Troup was an unqualified success. The Glaswegians, and many people from elsewhere, came to Green's Playhouse. GUEA minutes for 12 September 1938 record 1,800 present for the Sunday afternoon service, 3,500 at the Sunday evening service, and attendances of 800–1,000 at the weeknight meetings at the Tent Hall. Many were blessed with salvation and challenged to practical Christian living. There was money enough and spare to cover all expenses. A Christian lady told me that every time she hears Christians singing 'To God be the glory', she remembers the full-throated splendour of the praise in the Playhouse. Eye-witnesses have commented on the hush which fell over meetings when Harry Ironside was preaching sermons which often lasted over an hour. Harry Ironside started his tour at Templemore Hall, Belfast. Other campaigns were held in Kilmarnock and Aberdeen, and the tour finished with a ten-day series in Kingsway Hall, London. The Communists were very active at the time, and someone told Jock just before the pre-service prayer meeting at the Playhouse one night that they had commandeered the two front rows. Jock left the prayer meeting early, and went out to use his voice and body language to good effect. An eye-witness told how Jock stood at the end of the rows, feet apart like a Sumo wrestler, and arms folded on his chest, and told them how it was 'nice to see you in here tonight, lads – but NO NONSENSE!' (the final phrase in his 'open-air voice'). There was no trouble. The Playhouse episode was an illustration of the vigour, energy and faith of Jock Troup, and his inspired leadership at the Tent Hall. Bert Henry described him as a 'strong man of God', and he said, 'I mean strong – in every way!' In 1939 Jock did a preaching tour in Canada and America under the auspices of Moody Bible Institute, Chicago: 18 March – 2 April, Toronto; 3 April – 7 April, Hamilton, Ontario;

9 April – 23 April, Grand Rapids, Michigan; 30 April – 14 May, Detroit; 21 May – 4 June, Augusta, Georgia; 11 June – 25 June, Hawthorne, New Jersey.

8

The Tent Hall in the War Years

When Adolf Hitler's insatiable desire for 'Lebensraum' ('living-space') finally over-stretched even Neville Chamberlain's patience, and Britain declared war on Germany in 1939, Glasgow braced itself for action. The Glasgow/Clydebank area in the West of Scotland, and the Rosyth area in the East of Scotland, were bound to be key targets in any German offensive from the air, because of the shipbuilding, steel manufacture and naval interest. Jock Troup had been involved in the First World War and his heart went out to the service personnel who could be seen on Glasgow's streets. He mirrored the attitude of the Lord Jesus to the crowds; he saw them like sheep without a shepherd. Glasgow's Maryhill Barracks became a hive of training activity. Cowglen Hospital was used for billeting soldiers. Drill halls all over the city of Glasgow were commandeered to prepare men for fighting. Mrs Bella Calder remembers taking soup to the soldiers occupying the BTI building in Bothwell Street.

The physical condition of the men now called up was considerably better than at the turn of the century for the Boer War or in 1914 for the First World War. The high incidence of tuberculosis, bronchitis and chest complaints in 1901 had been reduced by the long-term public health improvements as a result of the Liberal reforms of 1906. Even in 1914 the numbers rejected for being undersized, underweight and generally unfit for active, or indeed any, military service, were appallingly high. The outbreak of World War II found the working class in Britain in better physical and psychological state than in 1914. In fact, a retrospective look from the twenty-first century makes us realize that the 1939–45 period was one of our best times nutritionally, despite shortages. Jock's Christian reaction was to welcome 'the strangers within our gates', and he immediately attempted to meet the spiritual needs of people who were separated from loved ones and would soon be in the firing line. He longed to help the lonely soldiers in a strange city and reach out with the Gospel to the unconverted lads all around. He inaugurated Supper services on Saturday and Sunday evenings, where the Gospel was faithfully proclaimed, and many were brought to a saving knowledge of the Lord. Soon after the outbreak of hostilities, he began issuing weekly Bulletins, and sent them all over the world, where allied troops were serving. He was an unashamed defender of the British Empire against Hitler, whom he regarded as an abominable tyrant. Here is a sample of his prose from 31 May 1940:

Dear Friend, The war horses have at last been let loose with all their horror and terror, and many of our brave boys have had to face the fierce brunt of the battle now raging. We are told daily the gravity of the situation, and yet there are still those who are unconcerned and unmoved. Those of us in attendance at the Tent Hall have always viewed the situation with gravity; war is no picnic, many of you, no doubt, have thought so far. You have been suddenly changed by the rude awakening of the last few days.

I am often asked what I think of the situation. My answer is 'serious, but praise God, not hopeless'...We may have to pass through the fire as a nation. Note what I say 'pass through' – we may have to be humbled as a people, because we certainly have not lived in accordance with the privileges which God has given us. Nevertheless, there are still many in our beloved land who have not bowed the knee to Baal; there are still more than ten righteous people left.

The response to the King's appeal for a day of national humiliation and prayer proved this. 'It is not mine to see what lies in store, I only know just what I need, not more, 'Tis mine not to be anxious or distressed, But simply rest'.

Let us therefore, face whatever may be before us with that calm confidence in God which has been so characteristic of our people in the past. Psalm 56: 9 'When I cry unto Thee, then shall mine enemies turn back: this I know, for God is for me'. It will cheer your heart to know that every department of the Lord's work is in good shape. I praise God for such a loyal and faithful band of workers. We give thanks to our Heavenly Father for answered prayer; some of our boys have already been rescued from the jaws of death. Unceasing prayer is being made for you all.

Christian love and greetings from myself and all associated with the work of the Hall.

Yours affectionately,

Jock Troup.

One of his slogans, quoted in a letter from a serviceman, was 'Hit Hitler Hard and Hurry Home!' The War turned ugly enough at home in the spring of 1941. From 13 till 15 March, German bombing raids left 1,083 people dead and 1,602 seriously injured in Glasgow and Clydebank. Clydebank was left with eight undamaged houses out of a housing stock of around 12,000. Further raids on 7 and 8 April left 64 dead and 71 injured, and in the first week in May 1941, 341 died and 312 were injured, with Greenock and Gourock the worst-hit areas.

The Tent Hall Christmas programme for 1941 contains photographs of tables crammed full of servicemen on Saturdays at 6 pm and Sundays at 7 pm, and states: 'We commenced this work among the men of His Majesty's Forces just over a year ago. About 14,000 have been provided with free meals, but best of all, about 300 of these dear boys have made a definite decision for Jesus Christ. This work has meant much extra labour and expense, the labour has been done mostly by our noble band of voluntary workers who contact the men on the streets and invite them to tea by means of an invitation card. Men from all the allied countries, and also from every part of the Empire have been our guests as we seek to carry out the Scriptural injunction 'Extend ungrudging hospitality towards one another'. His concern for the spiritual needs of the troops led Jock to seek funding from the Christian public to finance the opening of a refuge for them in the city. Under the auspices of the GUEA, the Opening Ceremony of the Moody and Sankey Rest Rooms for Service Men took place at 191 (2 up) Argyle Street, Glasgow on Saturday, 7 November 1942 at 3 o'clock. The chairman was the Rt Hon. Lord Maclay, PC, LLD, and the premises were opened by Captain Walter Hughes, Chaplain to the Royal Canadian Forces. What a haven of rest and joy these rooms proved to be, a Christian alternative to the boozy and the tawdry. The troops loved this facility, and referred to the Rest Rooms often in their letters. What did the Superintendent do to find a haven of rest? During the earlier years of the War, Jock was able to make his occasional escape from the crushing responsibilities of the Tent Hall ministry. This was rarely possible after the Rest Rooms opened, because they were open from 10 am until 10 pm, seven days a week, and Jock found himself regularly implicated in the running of the place. His favourite bolt-hole when he escaped was Inverness, where his dear friend John MacBeath had become the minister of the Baptist Church, and served the Lord there from 1940 until 1959. They had been friends since childhood, and John MacBeath had been minister of Harper Memorial Baptist Church in Glasgow from 1936 until 1940, during Jock's earlier years at the Tent Hall. John MacBeath was an outstanding man, who became President of the Baptist Union of Scotland in 1956. (The title of his Presidential address was 'Revival'.) Jock and John were known as 'the two Jocks', and occasionally sang duets. People in Avoch Congregational Church remembered them singing 'Down at the Bottom of the Deep Blue Sea', a ditty with which the author is not familiar.

The main interest which drew Jock to Inverness was down at the bottom of the deep blue river – fishing. Mrs Amelia MacBeath told me that Jock used to arrive for the evening meal, after which they would 'put the world right', and next morning take off to some Highland stream, where they would exercise their fishing skills, and enjoy her packed lunches. Jock's natural impatience prevented him from ever being a good fisherman, but the scenery, the companionship, the ritual and the freedom did them both good. On one occasion, Jock arrived in Inverness at short notice, and insisted that he would supply the lunch. When they got to the fishing ground, after an amazingly short period at the fishing, Jock said they should stop for lunch. The 'lunch' was a packet of digestive biscuits shared between them, and a packet of cream cheese wedges! John MacBeath insisted that all future meals should be supplied by Amelia!

On a personal note, Jock's family have kindly let me have access to letters written to him, and to Mrs Troup and the children during the Second World War. I do not know what became of most of the people who wrote, and I have no desire to cause any distress to relatives of the dead, but I think the letters written to him authenticate the ministry of the Tent Hall and of Jock Troup in the War years, and deserve to be shared with others. The letters also demonstrate the strengthening role of the people of God in the lives of those servicemen and women who passed through Glasgow during the War, and the warm affection in the hearts of these short-term visitors for the city and its kind-hearted people. The letters also bear out Martin Luther's comment on the relationship between grace and works. 'Good works do not make a good man; but a good man does good works.'

Here was one of God's servants who could legitimately have avoided a responsibility, but who took it on for the benefit and blessing of service personnel. He sent them weekly Bulletins. It is obvious from the contents of the letters that he wrote to many of them personally, and included the Tent Hall workers in sending out parcels containing books, soap and other commodities. To give one specific example, Mrs Troup bought underclothing and sent it to a serviceman admitted to hospital – all the tasks that Jesus would have done.

There are ninety-four letters from servicemen and women. They are nearly all from the lower echelons of military society – privates, sappers, gunners, ordinary seamen, craftsman, and leading aircraftmen. The branches of the services represented is very wide. There are people from the Scottish regiments, as you would expect – Gordon Highlanders, Seaforth Highlanders and the Black Watch. There are people from the Royal Army Medical Corps, Royal Artillery, Royal Engineers, Royal Electrical and Mechanical Engineers, Royal Army Service Corps, Pioneer Corps, Royal Marines, Green Howards, Royal Australian Air Force, Royal Air Force and the Royal Navy. Where did the letters come from? Some came from Britain – RAF Cranwell, and Oakham in Rutland, Marston Moor in Yorkshire, and the Royal Artillery Batteries at Ipswich and Harwich. Some addresses are vague, or further afield: 'Somewhere in France', Tunisia, North Africa, RAF West African Forces, Italy, India, and South East Asia. Some are written on Air Mail Letter Cards, some on Moody and Sankey Rest Rooms notepaper, others on the strict forces letter forms. As old Thomas Guthrie says, in another connection, (apologizing for the poor quality of God's preachers): 'when you receive a good message from a far land, you do not complain about the quality of the paper!' In a few cases, people obtained the help of a friend because they weren't good at spelling or unused to writing. This all adds to the reality and authenticity of what they have to say. They are people who probably didn't usually write letters, but who felt they had to respond to kindness shown. Like the proportionate response to Jesus cleansing the lepers, we are probably correct in assuming that behind the number who wrote there was a much larger number who received but did not write! The letters reveal a warmth about Glasgow and Glaswegians, and the Tent Hall and Jock Troup. The references to his wife and children indicate the ministry that Mrs Troup exercised in the background.

Another factor is that we are frequently reading responses from people under military threat, often underplaying the danger and being deliberately restrained in the information they give about themselves and their location. To set the scene by quotations from some of the soldiers who were in action, consider these true statements:'I feel I have been living on borrowed time since I was twenty years of age. The casualties out of a battalion strength of 800 were 600 killed or wounded.' 'We were forever pulling boys up off the ground, slapping their faces and saying 'Wake up, keep going!' Because once you'd fallen asleep, you'd had it.''For

Argylls and Gordons captured by the Japanese there were no camp concerts, Red Cross parcels, or letters from home'. In many of the letters we have, people do not even give a Christian name – they quote their service number, surname and initials, because that is how they had been trained. All the letters can be fitted into the period from October 1943 until October 1944. Some minor tinkering with spelling and grammar has taken place.

What kind of things do they say? Some paint on a broad canvas. Leading Aircraftman (LAC) R. with the Air Force in Italy writes, two days before the Allies broke through German defence lines along the River Volturno: 'Let us pray that our statesmen will be guided by the good Lord to make full use of this Victory and give their people the things which we feel they ought to have, freedom in everything'. A letter from Corporal Mary P. illustrates the ubiquity of the Bulletins and the ministry of Mrs Troup:

> Dear Mrs Troup, at last I am finding time to scribble you a line to show my appreciation of the 'bulletin'. The reason I am writing to you and not Mr Troup, is, that it is always your writing that is on the envelope and to my surprise today it was strange hand-writing, so I do hope that you are alright. A brother in the Lord who is now in North Africa wrote

to me last week with very interesting news, he incidentally used to get the bulletin from me, and then passed it on to his wife after reading. He was sitting in a canteen abroad a few weeks ago, and on the table nearby he lifted a sheet of paper to find that it was a weekly bulletin from the Tent, and he said he nearly fell through his chair. He was not surprised to learn that the soldier sitting beside him was a child of the same wonderful Saviour, and belonged to the Salvation Army. I thought that was really great! Anyway, it cheered my heart.

RAF man LAC Stanley M. writes shortly before the Allies launched a heavy assault on Monte Cassino, Italy:

Just a few lines in appreciation of the Bulletin which I am regularly receiving every week now. I look forward to every Friday now, as it is a great help to me. In my present situation, I am isolated from any place where meetings are held.

Lance-Corporal R. of the Green Howards:

Just a few lines to express my thanks for the book which I received the other week...I have read it and passed it on that others may see and know the work which had to be done before we could have our present-day Bible...I have heard your work for the service-men praised, and it was by an Englishman who is a Roman Catholic. He did his training at Maryhill Barracks, Glasgow, and was invited to the Tent Hall, and spent a few nights there.

Some of the lads seem to have been one-man evangelistic crusades! Here is LAC Joe C. writing from India as if there weren't a War on. In fact, the South East Asia Command, under its Supreme Commander, Lord Louis Mountbatten, came into being in August 1943. The role of the RAF was vital in supplying the Chinese using 'the Hump Route', at 23,000 feet across the Himalayas, flying in 20,000 tons a month. They, with the US Air Force, in a ratio of one to four, were also dropping large numbers of Allied troops, the Fourteenth Army (British, Indian, Gurkha and African) behind enemy lines in Burma, totalling 315,000 reinforcements, with 110,000 casualties flown out. The Chindits received over 95 per cent of their supplies by air. Vital battles were fought at Kohima and Imphal from 3 April until 31 May 1944. Sunday 23 April 1944:

My Dear Jock, Christian greetings! I am writing you under some slight difficulties; the temperature is 118 degrees F, my only attire is a pair of shorts, yet I am simply bathed in perspiration, not to speak of all the multitude of flies etc... For some time now, I have been responsible for organising the men for an Evening Service in town, about seven miles away. The CO has been kind in giving us this privilege. Some Sundays I have a convoy of three transports for the service...as we return to camp, it would do your heart good to hear the men on the transport singing 'He lives', 'Turn your eyes upon Jesus', 'He is Mine', etc. How Frank (my Christian friend) and I feel that the Lord has placed us here to give the men the Gospel.

Here he comes again! It is 1 June 1944 and the letter is written from India. (The Allies were busy elsewhere, dropping 8,000 tons of bombs on German coastal positions centred on Boulogne on 4 June.)

My Dear Jock,
Greetings in the Lord's Name! Yes! Despite the difficulties of life out here, and hard going, I feel abundantly happy in Him, and praise Him for His manifold blessings! The Air Ministry build and furnish cinemas on the camps, but no church, so with the CO's permission and materials, we built a church. For the time being, we became bricklayers, joiners and plasterers, etc., and now it would do your heart good if you could see our little

church. Another Christian brother and I organized a two-week evangelistic campaign in the camp. It meant a good deal of hard work, especially in temperatures of 117 degrees F, but the Lord rewarded our efforts. The attendances were not large, but quite a number of men found the Lord.

One night, five men came right out and said that they felt they should give themselves to Jesus. Our hearts burned within us as we helped them from the Word, and they yielded to Him. Pray for these boys, because the duties of service life sometimes makes it impossible to keep in touch with them. Scores of others like Nicodemus have come to ask more about the way of life... A good number of men who were nominal Christians and afraid to witness have now come forward and joined us, so that I now have about twenty Christians ready to witness for Jesus. I obtained permission to have a Bible Study Class on Saturday evenings... A Gospel meeting is conducted on Thursday evenings, so you see, dear brother, I have plenty to do, but my soul has been refreshed.

Private Harry W. of the Royal Army Service Corps reveals the uncertainties of life in wartime, and reflects the view shared by every Glaswegian that Glasgow is the centre of the world:

Revival Man

I am wondering where I shall wake up
tomorrow morning. This place is about eight
miles nearer Glasgow, but wish we were only
eight miles away, as I remember the
enjoyment at those meetings. We could see
the presence of Jesus in the crowd...Thank
God for the Tent Hall. I wish there were more
such places about. Those songs, 'He is mine',
'Meeting in the Air', etc., are quite simple,
and seem to stir one's heart. The highbrow
stuff in some churches is a waste of time.
Surely Jesus does not want all that
formality...I would like to send best wishes
to you all. One consolation is that every day
passed is one nearer to our dear Lord.

Some letters show insight and sympathy for
the hard work done by Jock and the writers try
to encourage him. Craftsman Willy of the
Royal Electrical and Mechanical Engineers
writes on Salvation Army notepaper, a day
before British and Canadian forces began a new
offensive South of Caen in France:

I grieve to hear the work is getting too much
for you, hope in your new partner, that more
rest will come to you. The little time it was
my privilege to spend in the warmest-hearted
city in Scotland, aye maybe Great Britain
come to that, I noticed you were a very active
firebrand evangelist, admired your spirit. You

182

are well known, Jock, among the boys. Take care of yourself, but for me to tell you that is a waste of time, you're a fighter like St Paul. You say Mr Moody's favourite text was, 'he that doeth the will of the Lord abideth for ever', yes that's true, or Easter Sunday is a myth. I love Easter and its real beauty and lightness of heart. To those who love God and believe in Him, the trials and loneliness of today we can endure, for death cannot defeat the Victory of Easter, up from the grave He arose with a mighty triumph o'er His foes.

Cheerio Jock, God bless you and yours.

Some soldiers write straight from the heart about their spiritual pilgrimage, like Private David McE. of the Pioneer Corps, writing from North Africa on the day significant things were happening elsewhere (British and Polish troops captured Cassino, in Italy) :

Just a few lines to let you know that I was born again in the Tolbooth Mission, Glasgow, the time Mr Munro was Supt, but I wandered far away from God, but thank God that He spared me to come back again into the Fold, as He is merciful... I will tell you how I came back. I came to North Africa, and I got down on my knees in my bivouac in a place called Bougie.. there was joy in heaven over me returning and by the grace of God I mean to go on. I know it is very hard to be a Christian

in the Army, but glory to God, He can keep
you anywhere. When I come home, I mean
to come and see you, for many times I went
to your late prayer meeting on a Friday night
till midnight, and I never enjoyed life so much
as I did then, not a penny in my pocket, but
Christ in my heart. I thank God I have the
same joy now, and by his grace I mean to go
on.

Gunner Arnold R. of the Royal Artillery
writes from the Middle East on the day when
the RAF set a new record for a single raid,
dropping 4,500 tons of bombs on Germany for
Hitler's fifty-fifth birthday:

Out here it is great, but nothing like Bonnie
Scotland. How I long for a glimpse of dear
old Glasgow and the old Tent Hall, the singing
and the texts. Please God it won't be long
now. There will be many vacant places, **but
none where Jesus is.**

Private Stan of the Royal Army Medical
Corps wonders at his recall from Italy (May 2
1944), and writes:

Although the eyes of the world are upon the
amount of arms at our disposal, we look away
from them to God, and if it pleases Him, he
can deliver us from this conflict, without the

necessity of a lot more bloodshed. May He keep us from limiting His power, and from glorying in our own or our country's material power. 'But let him that glorieth, glory in this: that he understandeth and knoweth that I am the Lord' (Jeremiah 9:23–24).

Private Rudolph K. of the Royal Canadian Army Medical Corps marvels at Jock Troup's personal interest and prayers, on the day after the RAF got specific, pinpointing and bombing a single target, the Air Ministry at the Hague. Writing on Salvation Army notepaper headed 'On Active Service with the Canadian Forces', he writes:

Quite unexpectedly, I received birthday greetings from you, and really was glad to see you still remember me personally. I can't recollect how you got to know when my birthday is, anyway you know it. Thank you so much for your love and above everything I'm glad to be remembered in your prayers. The Christian men in the Forces are surely in need to be brought before the Throne of Grace. We are not only exposed to dangers from enemy shellfire. Our biggest enemy is the devil making assaults by means of tempting us, using his slaves as agitators and we have constantly to watch ourselves if we want to live a just and sober life...So glad to hear the Lord is blessing the work at the Tent Hall, and is manifesting His saving power . 'Redeem the time for the days are evil...'

Royal Marine Ben S has become involved in open-air witness.

I've adopted a new means of testifying in open-air meetings. Instead of just saying 'I'm glad I'm saved, Amen etc, I use the text Romans 1: 15-16, and it's great to see the difference. The people just stand and LISTEN when they see a Royal Marine saying that it is high time they were saved.

Some of the troops were quite demanding! Sapper D. must have been keen to do some evangelizing. He writes:

Dear Sirs, I would be pleased if you can oblige me by sending me some more cards like this one and let me know by return if you can spare at least 320. I think that will be enough, and if not, I will write and let you know.

Now for news of globetrotting soap...LAC Alfred W. of the RAF writes:

Dear Mr Troup, I take this opportunity of writing to you again in acknowledgment of the weekly bulletins still being received regularly, and also for the parcel of soap etc., received today, which seems to have travelled over nearly half the world, according to all the addresses written thereon. Please convey my sincere thanks to the workers of the Tent Hall for all their continued kindness.

Lieutenant Gordon N. of the British Cadre of the 3 Italian Pack Tpt Coy looks forward from Italy :

I would like to thank you again for your prayers which are being answered out here in Italy. It is our desire that we, if God permit, should come home more fitted to live Christ amongst our fellows at home, and to be able to bear witness to the amazing power and protection that God gives to those who put their trust in Him. During times of difficulty God has been a mighty Deliverer.

Private David McE. of the Pioneer Corps (see his earlier letter about his conversion in the Tolbooth Mission) writes movingly of God's help and his testimony about the Bible:

Well brother, I may tell you that I am a Volunteer. I was in France in 1940 and after coming home, I went to North Africa and from there to Italy, and I was at Anzio beach-head, but thank God my Heavenly Father was with me. Jesus never leaves you. I thank Him for bringing me through hell, and giving me everlasting life. By His grace I mean to go on, and when this war is finished I will come and see you and get down to those happy late-night prayer meetings.

I may tell you I was reading the Word of God at Anzio and one of my soldiers came forward and said 'David, you are only reading that Bible because you are in a very bad place because Jerry is shelling us. When you get away from here you will forget all about it'. Well, I got away from it through the power of God and I spoke to that lad and I told him I am still reading God's Word, and by His grace I mean to go on. Here is a little prayer I got off one of the lads before he was killed. 'Guard us O Lord from every danger both to body and soul, and cover our weakness in the shadow of Thy strength. Through Jesus Christ our Lord, Amen.'

Craftsman Tom F. of the Royal Electrical and Mechanical Engineers writes confidently from North Africa on 1 June 1944:

Things have been going well and we thank and praise God for what has been gained so far, and trust that he will enable us to completely defeat the enemy. May He grant a speedy and righteous peace. Victory is of the Lord...may this truth be recognized by

our leaders and people in these days. Truly
we would have been in a terrible state had
not the Lord intervened and helped us... I do
pray that the Lord will richly bless His Word,
Work and Workers in the Tent Hall...Glad
to read that the Open-Air is still going on at
Glasgow Cross. May the Lord greatly bless
this witness.

The Jock Troup communications system was a
great comfort to Private J.E.W. of the Royal
Army Medical Corps, the day before the first
V-1 bomb landed in England :

Yours was the first letter I received when we
landed in France, and we all knew that we
had your prayers. We have to thank God that
He has kept us safe from all harm. It was
very hard at first, but we are doing not so
bad. Now we have one chap in our ward from
Glasgow. He is called Mr McRoberts, of
Carmyle, Glasgow. Perhaps you could do me
a favour and let his folks know that he is doing
very nicely.

Aircraftsman J.P.L. of RAF Chigwell in Essex
had a prayer request:

I would like for all who attend the Prayer
Meeting to keep us in remembrance before
the Throne of Grace. I will be going overseas

shortly as the Second Front has been opened.
I am under training at the moment and in the
best of health.

Private David McE. of the Pioneer Corps also
had prayer requests:

I pray that God will spare my body and soul
to go back to my wife and family in Bonnie
Scotland. I may tell you I have a son eighteen
years of age away to France as he volunteered
to go. Will you please remember him in your
prayers as he is not a Christian.

Sapper John McK. of the Royal Engineers had
a preaching request from the Middle East:

It is many moons since I last wrote to you,
and I know that you will forgive me for not
writing as I am kept fairly busy on the docks
over here loading and unloading ships for
what I hope will spell Victory for us all some
bright day, and like yourself I hope the final
shot will be fired soon. Jock, should I ever be
back in dear auld Scotland again, then I would
like very much if you would do me a great
favour and just let me speak from the pulpit
for just ten short minutes and I am quite sure
that you would not regret it. Jock, I hope
and pray that God's blessing may continue
to be with you at all times.

There seems to have been an interest in Bibles. Private Jake R. from Canada tells:

> I received nineteen New Testaments from the Gideons in Toronto three weeks ago. They are the best I have ever seen for the Forces. They went like hot cakes! I did very little scouting around to see who didn't have any, as both officers and men came to me for a copy, of their own free will. Praise God! They are feeling their need now that the battle-fields are near. I have ordered another forty more. I only pray that as they read their eyes may be opened to see the Lamb of God.

In the same letter, Jake marvels at the Tent Hall grapevine:

> I had a very nice surprise when I received a lovely birthday card from you all. I treasure it dearly – its words are very fitting. It is mysterious to me as to how you knew when my birthday was?

Private David F. writes a forward-looking letter from the Infantry Battalion HQ:

> I do trust that our nation won't forget God in these crucial days, but will follow King George's lead and seek His face diligently, and this war will be over earlier than we think possible.. How apt we all are to forget the

Lord until times like these come upon us, but I hope that in the days ahead we'll remember Him more and give Him the pre-eminence in our lives. We are now into the final phase of the war in Europe, and Hitler's days of power are fast coming to a close...it will be home for all the lads, and we won't be sorry either, as we've had enough journeying about to last us a lifetime...may the Lord make the old Tent a real place of blessing to all who enter its doors.

Although it is July 1944, and Private H.N. of the Pioneer Corps has survived the Allied invasion of Europe at the Normandy landings, he is keen to learn!:

The language here is hard to master, and I'm wondering if there's an old French dictionary lying around the Tent Hall.

Royal Navy Flotilla staff man A.J. looks back with gratitude:

Eighteen months ago I was never known in Glasgow, and I never was dreaming of the very happy times the Lord had planned I should have there...the time I spent with you in the early summer of 1943 were eight of the best I've spent in the Navy. Over and over again I remember giving my testimony in the Tent Hall in front of a crowd. I've never witnessed before in a Gospel meeting. Also in the Services Tea Meeting, and in the open-air meetings in Argyle Street and in the Moody and Sankey Rest Rooms in Argyle Street, these were weeks I shan't forget.

Private Ted S. of the Pioneer Corps has a difficult time witnessing:

There seems very little interest with the lads, but we must pray for them all to be brought to the light of Christ, if it be His will. That Saturday night, Jock, when you led me to Christ, that was the best thing you ever did for me.

At the risk of wearying the reader if we continue, the case rests. Jock, Mrs Troup, and the workers of the Tent Hall honoured God in their ministry to the forces during the Second World War. And the whole story has still to be told... His ministry among the troops was motivated by the same revival urge of the soul-winner which had stayed with him since 1921, epitomized in the chorus sometimes attributed to Jock, but really written by Will Houghton:

Lead me to some soul today,
Teach me Lord just what to say,
Friends of mine are lost in sin,
And cannot find their way.

Few there are who seem to care,
And few there are who pray.
Melt my heart, and fill my life,
Give me some soul today.

Jock spoke about soul-winning when he was asked to address a rally of evangelical troops from Canada in February 1944 in London. He based his talk on the parables of Matthew 22 and Luke 14. He said: 'Here is the message that is very much needed today among the Lord's people, because as I said at the beginning there is no work under God's heaven that I know of that can bring more discouragement in the heart of a man or a woman than the Lord's work. Don't run away with the idea that it is easy! The man who runs away with the idea that God's work is easy – that winning souls is easy – is living in a fool's paradise. As Captain Reginald Wallis used to put it so aptly "Pentecost is plenty cost". The man or woman who will go all the way with God has got to measure up with the fact that God Almighty will not countenance discouragement in the heart of any of His people. The truest thing that D.L. Moody ever said was this, "God can never do anything with a man who becomes discouraged". He has no time nor place for discouragement in His programme. Yet I speak the truth and lie not, there is not a master stroke the devil has used oftener, and with greater effect in the lives of the Lord's people than that thing called discouragement. Here is the antidote – He called His servants together – these servants are put out in relays. The servants are put out to gather all, as many as they could, both good and bad, to bring them in. That is our business in life and there is no discrimination – "For God so loved the *world*". Have you ever tried this business? It is not easy, is it? When you go out without any thought of discrimination as to whom you should call upon, sometimes the reaction is just what we have in the parable. They did not want to come. God never tires of sending us out. "Go", He says, "into all the world". This is our business, but I have heard some people having a skit at mass evangelism. You hear another group saying "I don't like the emotional type" well, I don't like the dead type! I don't believe it is in God's programme. They say "we can't have anything to do with sensationalism". No – they have never produced anything that would cause a sensation. When men and women get born again, it is a sensation! We are not in this business alone. It is a lonely business if you are; but I want to tell you that it is the best business on God's earth when a man or a woman gets linked up with the Holy Ghost. One of the reasons why the work is so dead and so dull and so discouraging today is because men and women are not aware that there is a Holy Ghost.

During the War years, there was a steady stream of service people coming to faith in Christ through the ministry of the Tent Hall. We must not minimize the work done by the wonderful background people who provided huge quantities of food, manned the Rest rooms and organized the sending of parcels and letters, prepared bulletins, and organized the busy crowds. But at the heart of the work was the revival man, leading folk to Christ. (The Christmas programme for 1941 says at least 300 members of the Forces came to the Lord in the first year of the War). There was an interlude of sorts in May 1944, when Jock went on an evangelistic campaign to Liverpool, and his preaching was greatly blessed. I have some letters which indicate this, and a lady's concern about Jock straining his voice.

From E.A.E. Hopkinson, St Paul's Vicarage, Kirkdale, Liverpool, Joint Secretary of the Liverpool Convention Evangelistic Campaign:

Dear Mr Troup,
Thank you so much for your kind and encouraging letter. I personally feel delighted to have met you and had such glorious fellowship in the Gospel. The Campaign for

our City was such a great inspiration, and Heaven is the richer for those who have come from the darkness of sin to the marvellous light and liberty of the Gospel. We are expecting a great time at the Converts' Meeting, and we trust that all of them will grow in Grace, and give a burning witness to the Saviour whose precious blood has saved them. May God continue to bless and use you, and give you joy in winning others for Him.

Very kindest regards,

Yours very sincerely,

E.A.E. Hopkinson.

From John Belford, Chairman of Convention Council:

My Dear Mr Troup,

Just a note to say thank you for your visit to Liverpool. Upward of 200 passed through the Enquiry room, and no doubt many more accepted the Saviour in the Great Hall, or after leaving the meetings. To God be the glory. It was all worth while...

From Rev. Harold Carter of Liverpool City Mission, Convention Council Member:

My Dear Jock, I do praise God for the way He honoured and blessed your testimony because it was I who fought to get you here, and now I am not disappointed...

Revival Man

From Mrs Laura M:

Dear Mr Troup, Before you leave Liverpool
I should like to thank you for the great help I
received under your ministry at the
Convention some weeks ago. I have been a
Christian for four years now, but when you
pointed out, that memorable Monday, that
'Christ brooks no rival in the human heart' I
promised the Lord I would be consecrated to
him, and it has made all the difference. Thank
you very much...I'm sure these meetings must
be a great strain on you, speaking every night.
Your voice carries perfectly into every part
of the Hall, and you do not need to strain it.
If you were just to speak with just a little less
strain, we could hear equally well. You don't
mind my telling you, do you Mr Troup? You
see, I have had such a blessing from the Lord
through you that I consider myself somewhat
privileged.

Yours gratefully.

From a schoolgirl who felt free to write:

Dear Mr Troup,
I am writing this to thank you for the good
times you gave us at Liverpool. There was
only one thing wrong that is they didn't last
long enough. My little brother aged 8 has
just told me to tell you he enjoyed the two

meetings he came to. I only missed one meeting myself, so that meant I did no homework for a fortnight. I am thriteen and attend Moreton Gospel Hall. I have been saved since the beginning of 1942. Could you send me the words of Little Moses, please? .... I shall be very grateful if you send them. My little brother told me to tell you his name is David.

    Yours with Christian love,
        Olive Gibbs.

9

Heading for Home

The demands of the World War II years wrecked Jock's health. He had one spell of illness towards the end of the War, which in present-day terms would be called 'burn-out'. He resigned as Superintendent of the Tent Hall in 1945. His last Bulletin to the Tent Hall faithful summarizes things very well, and gives a splendid insight into his relationships with his colleagues in this huge work of God: *Weekly Bulletin* 16 August 1945.

Dear Friend,
Since this is my last Bulletin I feel I must make it somewhat different. I am nearing the close of my ministry as Superintendent of the Tent Hall and let me therefore render to all who have helped, their dues.

First, let me pay tribute to my Directors who, from the very commencement until now, have stood by me and given me every encouragement to get on with God's work. Not once did they seek to put a stumbling-block in my way; they have always acted as Christian gentlemen and have been sympathetic and kindly disposed towards any project to bring the Gospel to the needy multitudes of our city. I pray God that they may be wisely led in their appointment of my successor, and that the great evangelistic traditions of the Tent Hall may continue unhindered and unbroken.

Secondly, I must give honour to the noble band of unselfish and devoted Christian workers who have made the work of the Lord a real pleasure. I say without hesitation there is not their equal throughout the whole of Great Britain; without their prayerful support, passion for souls and enthusiasm for evangelism, the maintenance of the work would have been utterly impossible. Perhaps the following incident will give you some idea of how some of them feel for the salvation of their fellows. On one occasion we had an unfruitful period, there was no response to the appeal for two weekends and this seemed to be more than one of the prayer warriors could stand. He came to me and said: 'Mr Troup, don't you think there must be something wrong in the Hall and that we should set aside time for special prayer?' We did as he requested, and the response returned. If it were possible I would suggest that every young Christian in the City should spend some time in the work of the Hall. They would learn the holy art of personal work, and would also get ample scope for the development of public speaking gifts.

I dare not attempt to enumerate the names of individuals lest I should offend, yet I feel there are some who deserve special thanks. Let me begin with David Harrison our pianist, to whom I owe much. He has the uncommon gift of knowing how to play and how to pray. Usually those who know lots about musical harmony seem to be especially good at causing spiritual discord. How can I ever thank our Senior Choir Leader Mr Wilson, who throughout my periods of storm and calm has nobly stood by me. I shall always cherish the memory of his help and sweet fellowship. In the absence of our beloved brother Joe Campbell, the Junior Choir has been led by David Somerville, to whom I also give special praise. He has proved a real friend throughout and by his devotion to Christ and his dedication to the Lord's work it has been worthwhile to have known him. There is no part of the work that suffered more by the outbreak of war than the Orchestra. Nevertheless George Harrison the Leader, has stood by the work although alone many a time. I owe George special gratitude for the gracious manner in which he undertook the work as Chairman of the Poor Children's Dinner. As such, he has been responsible for the booking of speakers and the maintenance of order, no easy job in these days of unruly children. What shall I say about James McNee? One of the oldest workers in the Hall, and the man who is mainly responsible for the arrangement of workers throughout the work of the Hall. The smooth working of the Hall is the envy of many and has been commented on by all. It is mainly due to the alertness of Mr McNee in getting the right men for the job in times of emergency. While mentioning the work of Mr McNee, it would be well to remember our beloved leader of the Free Breakfast choir, Mr John MacDougall. His quiet unassuming Christian manner has endeared him to all, and he is an example of Christian consistency, having led this choir for over fifty years. We are truly proud of our band of Back-Court Workers, who throughout the years, in all kinds of weather, bring the message of good cheer to the dwellers in the cheerless atmosphere of our city centre. This band of young people have been under the leadership of Arthur Campbell who is one of the most spiritual young men I have met throughout my spiritual career. His open and loveable good nature has endeared him to all in the Hall. It is Arthur who has been responsible for the Missionary Offerings, as Secretary and Treasurer, our finances have climbed from the valley of humiliation to the heights of giving till it hurts. A work like that carried on in the Tent Hall where we cater for the needs of all, drunk or sober, moochers and mashers, rich and poor, demands physically strong and spiritually tactful men at the doors. This work has been ably carried out by Mr Joe Clark who, in spite of the most thankless job on earth, has carried on undaunted. The spectator is always good at throwing about unnecessary advice; he often seems to know but seldom seems to do.

Although our Secretary of the Association, Mr R.C. Brown has his hands full at Head Office, No. 64 Bothwell Street, he has always found time to prepare a helpful and well-studied message week by week for the Young People in the Bible Class. He has carried on this work for well over twenty years, and many of the Young People now serving in the Forces remember him with gratitude. All spiritual work is entirely dependent upon the prayers of the Lord's people and I dare not fail to make mention of one of the greatest warriors at the Throne of Grace I have yet met, Mr Willie Brown. His life of prayer and practice will always be an inspiration to me as I return to the field of evangelism. Now for the Women's side of the work. Is there another Women's Meeting anywhere that has such a great record as that of the Hall for getting a job done, for giving of their substance, for going to the help of others, and yes, for the grace of endurance throughout the war years? This marvellous piece of work for God and humanity has increased and abounded in every good work under the Leadership of Mrs Alex. Mullin. Her spirituality, sagacity and strength of Christian character has been a tower of strength to the dear old Grannies, Mothers and Maidens. God has indeed greatly blessed her work of faith and labour of love. In all my dealings with Mrs Mullin she has been both gracious and faithful and I sincerely thank her.

Next there is the work of the Girls' Class under the Leadership of Miss Annie Ralph. Although herself handicapped in more ways than most, she has been specially fitted for the work amongst the girls. God has endowed her with a most lovable nature, a gracious manner, an understanding spirit, and most of all, a real passion for prayer. Those associated with the Class hold Miss Ralph in the very highest esteem, and her patience and sympathy will always be a pleasant memory to me. I cannot forget those girls who have been so faithful and consistent in addressing the envelopes for the Bulletins week by week. In your name we acknowledge the debt of gratitude we owe them.

Last on the list, but by no means least on our list of honorary workers is our beloved sister, Mrs Jessie Dunbar. Mrs Dunbar is an absolute necessity to such a work as that of the Tent Hall. I doubt if there is another

woman in the length and breadth of our
beloved land who has such an uncanny insight
into the depths of human nature. I am certain
that Mrs Dunbar, although not versed in the
modern art of the much advertised highbrow
psychology, could teach some of its teachers
a thing or two. I am glad to have known her
and to have had her help in the work of the
Lord. Mr David Tweedie our Hall Keeper and
the man responsible for the catering and
cleansing of the Hall has not only been a great
help in the work, but has also been a staunch
friend. There is no Christian community on
this earth that has been better served; there is
no place of worship anywhere kept in a
cleaner condition; and there is no servant of
God who has been more faithful to the work
entrusted to him. Believe it or not, the GUEA
are mighty fortunate in having a Servant who
has such a minute care for its interests. Mr
James Haxton and I are really only getting to
know each other. As Assistant he has been
true blue and I feel that it is just a pity he is
over the fifty mark, or where else could the
Directors have looked for a successor? All
our dealings and doings have been sweet, and
during my illness Mr Haxton has been an
untold blessing and help. I pray God that he
may be long spared in the Lord's work.

In closing, again I say God bless you. I
shall always be interested in your welfare and
shall continually remember you at the Throne

of Grace. Christian Greetings and Love from all associated with the work of the Hall.

    Yours affectionately,
      Jock Troup.

He had to rest for a considerable period before getting his bearings. Katie, as ever, was his greatest supporter. Those who were observers of the family life consistently say that she had a calming influence on him. We have painted a picture of a fine Christian man whose character was stuffed full of endearing qualities as a result of the workings of God's grace in his life. However, this is not a hagiography. We must attempt to replicate Biblical method which paints its heroes honestly, 'warts an' all' as Oliver Cromwell instructed his portrait painter.

Jock had faults, like the rest of us. He was restless, impatient and at times intolerant. He hated waiting in queues! Bob Clapham tells how he and Jock went into a crowded fish-and-chip shop in Arbroath, and Jock asked the people in the queue, politely, whether they would allow him to go first! They did! Katie had to use every ounce of her skills to quieten him down after the feverish activity of the War years. For a Christian used to limelight, the platform and busy-ness, there is a thin line between what the psychologists call *'eu-stress'* (a manageable tension which helps us perform well, like a well-tuned violin string), and *distress,* which robs us of peace and causes us suffering because of the corroding effects of anxiety. His last Bulletin at the Tent Hall was dated 16 August 1945. Within a short period of time, the Christians pursued him for meetings and evangelistic campaigns. A letter came from T.T. Shields of Jarvis Street Baptist Church, Toronto, Canada, dated 9 August, with a tentative suggestion that Jock should take a month of meetings starting in September 1945.

In the month of June 1946, Jock took a series of meetings in the St George's Cross Tabernacle, from Sunday 9 June until Sunday 30 June under the general heading 'Topics for the Times'. On the first Sunday, the subjects were 'Blessed, but not Baptized', and 'Born, but not Born Again', followed by 'A Four Day Fight' on 'The Problem of Prayer', 'The Place of Prayer', 'The Partnership of Prayer' and 'Power through Prayer'. On Sunday 16 June the subjects were 'The Comforter and your Conflict' and 'The Comforter and your Conviction', followed by four talks on the Second Coming of Christ. On Sunday 23 June the subjects were 'Future Felicity of the Saved' and 'Fearful Fire for the Sinner', followed by four week-night talks on 'My Record and God's Remedy', 'Reasoning to Restore', 'Reluctant to Receive' and 'Running a Risk'. Sunday 30 June ended the sequence with 'A Ramble Through Romans' and 'Rest for the Restless'. There was a half-an-hour open-air testimony before each meeting, preceded by a short time of prayer. A special feature of the Campaign was 'Singing – solos, duets, trios, quartettes, augmented choir'.

Going further on in 1946, there were invitations to Central Baptist Church, Gary, Indiana (dated 21 June) and Waverley Road Baptist Church, Toronto (28 June). The Pastor, Captain Walter Hughes, MBE, BA, says: 'We have a rather strong organization here known as the Veterans' Christian Fellowship. They are most anxious that you should pay Canada a visit. You were a great friend and true counsellor to hundreds of our Canadian Servicemen and now as they are just settling down again into their own homes and churches, your ministry would come with special blessing. A strong itinerary will be arranged for you beginning in Ottawa at the commencement of November, Renton Baptist Church in Kitchener, Ontario, wrote on 1 July 1946, Calvary Baptist Church in Guelph, Ontario, on 5 July 1946, Central Baptist Church on 8 July 1946 and the Metropolitan Tabernacle of Ottawa on 8 July 1946. The Christian Commandos of Toronto wrote on 16 July 1946, and Forward Baptist Church of Toronto on 24 July 1946. He was associated with The Evangelization Society of London for a time. This inter-denominational organization was founded in 1864, thanks to the Christian generosity of people like Samuel Morley, a millionaire hosiery manufacturer.

On 7 October 1946 Jock (and Katie) signed an Agreement whereby he would serve the Society from 1 November 1946, for £350 per annum plus 15 per cent cost of living bonus. By this agreement the Evangelist must agree the Society's Basis of Belief, and notify them of any change in his views, and he must 'during his employment devote his whole time and service to the work of the Society.' The Evangelization Society minutes contain occasional references to Jock's activities in America, and the minute of 28 September 1951 says, 'Mr Troup seemed to feel a call to work in the Highlands of Scotland, and to this the Committee agreed. It was felt, however, that if he was to keep on crossing to America it would be difficult to retain him as a permanent member of the staff.' On 28 May 1953, the Society's minute under 'Evangelists' says: 'Mr Troup's visit to Canada was reported and leave of absence was granted him without pay, but he was to be reminded that there was a great need for his services in this country'.

Jock was certainly busy after the Canada invitations mentioned earlier were taken up. His diary for 1947 included the following: January in Newtonards, Northern Ireland; February in Annalong, Northern Ireland; March in Hawick, April in Porthcawl, Wales; June in Glasgow, July/August in Bangor, Northern Ireland; October in Southend-on-Sea, November in Montrose, and December in Arbroath. In 1948 he was in Perth in January, Newport, Wales, in February, Liverpool in April, Swansea, Wales, in May, Inverness Baptist Church in September, and the Gordon Mission, Aberdeen, in October.

The minute of Inverness Baptist Church Annual Business Meeting on 13 October 1948 reports:'To conclude a very memorable year (Fiftieth Anniversary of the opening of the church and Pastor's eighth anniversary) we experienced a time of real blessing during the campaign conducted in September by Mr Jock Troup, when quite a number had found the Saviour, backsliders had been restored, and God's own people had been revived and quickened'. Hugh Mitchell remembers the thrill he had as a boy, being asked to carry Mr Troup's Bible to the meetings.

Jock's 1949 bookings included work with the Faith Mission in Fort William in January, Belfast in February, Liverpool City Mission in March, Wigan and Bolton in April, Liverpool in May, Bangor, Northern Ireland, in July/August, Middlesborough, in September, Lerwick, Shetland, in October and Inverness in November.

In 1950 he had a sad and unsatisfactory year as an Associate Pastor in Texas. He made six trips in all to America. During the last of these, the Lord took him home – suddenly. Jock had always said that he wanted to die 'in harness', 'with his boots on', 'while I am preaching the Gospel'. 'I don't want to die in bed', he said. A few years before he died, he had been very ill when a blood vessel in his throat burst while he was preaching in the open air. The doctor advized him to take life very easy or he would only have two years to live. Jock responded by saying he would live his final years to the full. He wrote to two of his dearest friends, Bob Clapham and Peter Donald, in the closing weeks of his life. Peter got a letter in which Jock said, on reflection, that he felt he had been used and discarded by some Christians, and Bob got a card saying that Jock and Bob would come up from the Panama Canal to sail up the West coast of America, then they would travel to Canada.

Jock would preach, Bob would sing, Betty would play the piano and Katie would take up the collection! At the opening meeting of a six-day campaign in the Knox Presbyterian Church in Spokane, Washington, he had just begun his message on the interview between Nicodemus and Christ. He gave out the text, 'Ye must be born again', and in an instant with the words fresh on his lips, God's faithful soldier collapsed. His wife ran to the front and he managed to say 'Katie' before he died. He was dead within a couple of minutes of collapsing. It was Easter Sunday, 18 April 1954.

James Alexander Stewart quotes from the Knox Presbyterian Church Bulletin: 'The Rev. Jock Troup, who was scheduled to hold six evening meetings at our church, was called home to be with the Lord shortly after he had begun the first sermon in the series. Rev. Troup met with the church Session at seven o'clock for the pre-prayer session and outlined the sermon topics and plans for the series. In the opening of the evening service he had taught the congregation a chorus, the words of which were: 'Just a little longer and the trump of God shall sound, Just a little longer and we'll all be glory bound, Look away to heaven, your redemption draweth nigh, Just a little longer and we'll meet Him in the sky'. His best friend, Dr Peter

Connolly summed him up aptly: 'He was a preacher – a Gospel preacher – a rugged Gospel preacher. That very ruggedness revealed a rustic beauty in the Gospel message he preached, making people love both the preacher and the message he preached...Jock Troup, from the hour of his conversion, had a divine tongue put in his mouth and nothing but death could silence him...I cherished his memory – the memory of a man who was every inch a man – the memory of a saint who rejoiced in the adventurous programme of Jesus Christ – a man who never feared a human face and yet who, in the presence of his God knew himself to be dust and dirt. A prince in Israel has fallen, but he has laid aside his armour for a robe of spotless white, now with Jesus he is walking where the river sparkles bright'.

There are many routes we could take on the way to evaluating the life of 'the revival man'. We could say he was unique, a 'one-off', a man raised up for a specific purpose, and his activities and achievements have no bearing on today's church or today's Christians. He certainly gave evidence of the four ingredients of revival with which we set out on this study – prayer, fire, possession and glory. It would possibly be helpful to specify some points of contrast between his life and context, and the Christians and the church of the present time. Christians today tend to be either too separatist and absorbed in Christian things or church services to have anything to do with 'the world' – or too worldly to see any urgency about evangelizing the world. The biblical dimension of the world as an anti-God system has been sidestepped. Our evaluation of worldliness can be too simplistic, pinning it down to a check-list of negative activities. To Jock, the world was an arena for evangelism, and the church a rescue shop rather than a mutual admiration society. The services of the church, as far as he was concerned, should be there to attract and win lost people from a lost world. God was more glorified, therefore, in sinners getting saved, than in the church having a correct liturgy.

In recent decades we seem to have a centre of gravity in evangelism which is grounded on methods rather than holiness. In the world of 'spin', those who have the reputation of knowing how to do it can market their methods and do very well. It is helpful and healthy to learn from revival times that God's emphasis has been on holy people He has mastered, rather than clever methods we can master. It is natural, if not necessarily biblical, to settle for a 'quick fix'. Although people like Jock Troup could be ridiculed in some quarters for an eccentric, Arminian theology, it is doubtful whether he ever read the works of Jacobus Arminius. We do know this – Jock Troup had a protective zeal for God's glory and reputation. A journalist was once very critical and scathing in his tone, and asked Jock, 'Where do these revivals come from, anyhow?' Jock grasped the man firmly by the lapels of his jacket, and forced him to his knees. When he had him on his knees, he put his face close to the journalist's face, and whispered, 'they're from GOD, son'. We are told that sometimes his whispers were like thunderclaps! The reason why the journalist got such treatment was not that Jock was a bully, but that he was jealous for the honour of God, which had been demeaned by the journalist. Another point to note, which is linked to the blessing God gave him in his life, is that the Lord is more interested in personal holiness than theological correctness.

It is very easy in today's climate, to be browbeaten or overpowered because the church is in a more marginalized and defensive position. We become bland, sanitized and insipid in our comments and behaviour. Men like Jock Troup were people of raw courage, fearless in outspoken Christian testimony in any company. We have noted earlier that Jock had an eye to the future in terms of Christ's imminent return. This was one of the reasons he was reluctant to go to Bible College. He felt such a concern for the lost, what used to be called 'a passion for souls' that he wanted to use every available opportunity he had to witness to them, and preach the Gospel to them so that they could be saved before Christ returned. There isn't much of that kind of urgency around these days. We have lost our cutting edge, and we don't preach much about Christ's return. Another factor is that the majority of Christians today seem uncommitted to the cause of Christ and the calls of the church for Christian workers. A minister in a local fraternal described contemporary church-going as 'a non-contact winter sport'. When asked for an explanation, he said that, in general, people only attend church in the winter, and when they do, they do not want any real contact with the routines of Christian service. A lady once said with reference to a gathering called a 'Workers' Tea' being held in her place of worship: 'If it really was a Workers' Tea we could hold it in the vestry!' When we assess the lives of Jock Troup and the Tent Hall workers, we seem to fall far short of their standards of zeal and energy. One of the most convincing arguments for the Gospel as far as those who came into contact with him, was Jock Troup's sincere commitment to Christ which made him give himself to others. Robert Harper, a neighbour of the Blacks at Stirkoke, said, 'The trouble with Jock Troup was that he was over-burdened with a generous heart'. Such self-giving, seen in the most practical ways, by servicemen during the War, for example, gave the Gospel an authentic, wholesome flavour. The life of a man like Jock Troup is a spur to all of us. The great cloud of witnesses pictured in the opening passage of Hebrews chapter 12 are not merely like spectators in the stadium, but encouragers to those of us running the race. They 'egg us on' to run with steady endurance, 'looking to Jesus, the Pioneer and Perfecter of our faith'.

BIBLIOGRAPHY

GLASGOW

Checkland, S.G. *The UPAS Tree*. University of Glasgow Press. 1976.

Christ in the City. GUEA 1874–1974. Centenary Booklet. Paisley: Browns, Printers.

The Glasgow City Mission. A Short History. Written on the Occasion of its Centenary. 1926.

Linklater, Magnus and Robin Denniston (Ed.) Chambers *Anatomy of Scotland*. Edinburgh: Chambers Limited, 1992.

Peter, Bruce. *100 Years of Glasgow's Amazing Cinemas*. Edinburgh: Polygon, 1979.

Smout, T.C. *Cambridge Social History of Britain 1790-1950. Volume 1 –Regions and Communities*. Ed. E.M.L. Thomson. Cambridge University Press, 1990.

Worsdall, Frank. *Tenement – A Way of Life*. Edinburgh: Chambers, 1979.

Worsdall, Frank. *The City That Disappeared*. Molendinar Press, 1981.

THE NORTH

Butcher, David. *Following the Fishing*. Newton Abbot, London: Tops'l Books, 1987.

Foden, Frank. *Wick of the North*. North of Scotland Newspapers. (to mark the 160th anniversary of the John o'Groat Journal). *c.*1996.

Bibliography

Hughes, E.D. *What God Hath Wrought.* The Story of the YMCA Inverness.

Omand, Donald (Ed). *The Grampian Book.* The Northern Times Limited.

BIOGRAPHY

Barnes, Stanley. *All for Jesus – The Life of W.P. Nicholson.* Ambassador Productions. 1996.

Trophies of Grace – Peter Connolly. Crockery, 1931.

English, E.S. *HA Ironside – Ordained of the Lord.* New Jersey: Loizeaux Brothers, Neptune, 1976.

Graham, Billy. *Just As I Am.* Harper Collins Zondervan, 1997.

Handyside, James. *Portrait of a Master Craftsman – Raymond McKeown.* Ambassador Productions, 1987.

Mitchell, George. *Comfy Glasgow.* Tain: Christian Focus Publications, 1999.

REVIVAL

Buckley, Norma and June. *Landmark Visitor's Guide.* East Anglia.

Edwards, Brian. *Revival – A People Saturated With God.* Evangelical Press, 1990

Evans, Efion. *Revival Comes To Wales – The Story of the 1859 Revival.* Bridgend: Evangelical Press of Wales, 1986.

Evans, Efion. *The Welsh Revival of 1904.* Bridgend: Evangelical Press of Wales, 1987.

Fawcett, Arthur. *The Cambuslang Revival.* Banner of Truth, 1971.

Ferguson, John (Ed.) *When God Came Down. An Account of the North Uist Revival.* Lewis Recordings, North Kessock, 2000.

Fleming, William. *If My People...* Tain: Christian Focus Publications, 1999.

Gibson, William. *The Year of Grace. A History of the 1859 Ulster Revival.* Ambassador Productions, 1981.

Govan, I.R. *Spirit of Revival.* Faith Mission. 3rd ed. 1960.

Griffen, Stanley. C. *A Forgotten Revival. East Anglia and NE Scotland 1921.* Day One Publications.

Hood, Paxton. *Portraits of the Great Eighteenth Century Revival.* Ambassador Productions Ltd.

Jowett, J.H. *The Preacher : His Life and Work.* Grand Rapids: Baker Book House, 1968.

Lloyd-Jones, D.M. *Revival.* London: Pickering, 1986.

Meek, Donald. *'Fishers of Men: The 1921 Religious Revival – Its Cause, Context and Transmission'.* Scottish Bulletin of Evangelical Theology, 17. Spring 1999.

Paisley, I.R.K. *The 'Fifty-Nine Revival'.* Martyrs' Memorial Free Presbyterian, 1981.

Ritchie, Jackie. *Floods Upon the Dry Ground.* Peterhead Offset Printers, 1983.

Stedman, Ray. *Body Life*. Regal Books, Ventura, California. 2ⁿᵈ ed. 1972.

Stewart, J.A. *Evangelism Without Apology*. Grand Rapids: Kregel, 1960.

Stewart, J.A. *Our Beloved Jock. The Story of a Revivalist Fisherman*. Philadelphia:Revival Literature.

Stott, J.R.W. *The Preacher's Portrait*. Grand Rapids: Eerdmans, 1961.

Whittaker, Colin. *Great Revivals*. London: Pickering. Revised Edition, 1984.

Skevington-Wood, A. *The Inextinguishable Blaze*. Paternoster Press, 1960.

WAR

Badsey, Stephen. *D-Day From the Normandy Beaches to the Liberation of France*. London: Tiger Books International, 1993.

Churchill, W.S. *History of the Second World War*. London: Cassell, 1980.

Mercer, Derek (Ed. in Chief). *Chronicle of the Twentieth Century*. Longman, 1988

Robertson, Seona and Wilson, Les. *Scotland's War*. Edinburgh and London: Mainstream Publishing, 1995.

Young, Peter. *World War II*. London: Tiger Books International, 1980.

Badsey, Stephen. *D-Day From the Normandy Beaches to the Liberation of France*. London: Tiger Books International, 1993.

JOCK TROUP'S story is quite simply extraordinary. From a childhood in the Far north of Scotland he went to work in the fishing industry and then on to service in the First World War. It was during the war that the major turning point in Jock's life arrived - his conversion.

Jock went on to become an Evangelist, but no ordinary Evangelist. To quote a neighbour *'he had huge hands. He could pick up a fully inflated football easily with one hand. He had sixteen-inch biceps, un-expanded, and a neck like a prize bull'*, and to match this formidable physical presence he had a fire for reaching the lost with the Gospel.

George Mitchell gives fascinating insights into the lives of the fisher folk on the east coast of Scotland, and Glasgow life in Jock Troup's time. He includes many testimonies of those influenced through the ministry of Jock Troup and looks at the ingredients of revival, providing a useful lesson to the Church today.

Dr. George Mitchell is pastor of Castle Street Baptist Church in Inverness, Scotland. Author of *Chained and Cheerful: Paul's Letter to the Philippians* ISBN 1 185792 666 8 (Published 2001), his autobiography, *Comfy Glasgow* ISBN 1 85792 444 4, was published in 1999 and was a best seller.